WHAT PEOPLE ARE

THE CASE FOR

Gentle and respectful, and at the same time rigorously logical,
Dillon's argument shows why philosophers, theologians, and
thinking people of all kinds, should take polytheism seriously. If
future generations say that pagan philosophers made a
comeback in the 21st century, they shall say Dillon was among
the first, and among the best.
Brendan Myers, author of *The Earth, The Gods, and The Soul: A
History of Pagan Philosophy*

For centuries now, most discussions of deity in the Western
world have pretended that the only available choices are one god
or none at all, in an attempt to erase the oldest and most widely
embraced option in world religions – polytheism, belief in many
gods. Steven Dillon's new study *The Case for Polytheism* is a
thoughtful and incisive exploration of polytheist belief as a live
option for modern people.
John Michael Greer, author of *A World Full of Gods: An Inquiry
into Polytheism*

The Case
for Polytheism

The Case
for Polytheism

Steven Dillon

BOOKS

Winchester, UK
Washington, USA

First published by iff Books, 2015
iff Books is an imprint of John Hunt Publishing Ltd., Laurel House, Station Approach,
Alresford, Hants, SO24 9JH, UK
office1@jhpbooks.net
www.johnhuntpublishing.com
www.iff-books.com

For distributor details and how to order please visit the 'Ordering' section on our website.

Text copyright: Steven Dillon 2014

ISBN: 978 1 78279 735 7

A CIP catalogue record for this book is available from the British Library.

Design: Lee Nash

Printed and bound by CPI Group (UK) Ltd, Croydon, CR0 4YY

We operate a distinctive and ethical publishing philosophy in all
areas of our business, from our global network of authors to
production and worldwide distribution.

CONTENTS

Acknowledgments

This book has been several years in the making and I am grateful to everyone who has encouraged me to continue and taken the time to read drafts as well as share insights. In particular Andrew Johnson, whose style of philosophy I have tried to emulate ever since encountering it, and my wife, whose feedback and support have been invaluable to me.

I dedicate this book to Lune: you've always been the only proof I've ever needed.

Chapter 1

What is a God?

Preliminary Thoughts

Yes, home they went, and all things beautiful,
All things high they took with them,
All colours, all the sounds of life,
And for us remained only the de-souled Word.
Torn out of the time-flood, they hover,
Saved, on the heights of Pindus.
What shall live immortal in song
In life is bound to go under.[1]

This is the final stanza of 'The Gods of Greece' by Friedrich von Schiller, who in excellent romanticist fashion mourns the death of the gods and the world they represented, slain by reason or the 'de-souled Word'. This seems to embody a common sentiment nowadays: human reason has decommissioned many ancient ideas, and polytheism is one of them.

But from the time I first read this, my mind revolted against it. The polytheism of ancient paganism implied a world full of mystery and adventure, and struck me as interesting and beautiful. Yet I simply could not bring myself to believe it. In fact, I sincerely albeit begrudgingly thought it was false, and even studied to be a Catholic priest for a few years. I could only dream about being pagan at this point in my life.[2] However, the time sometimes comes when our minds are seized and directed in unpredictable ways, and that time came for me with neither haste nor delay.

The following investigation is an exercise in natural theology. A natural theology is just a systematic attempt 'to prove or show to be probable the existence of God or gods, and to acquire knowledge about them, on the basis of evidence or premises that can be accepted by non-believers, such as empirical knowledge about the natural world.[3]

For centuries now natural theology has been dominated by monotheists. Whether arguing from the apparently fine-tuned initial conditions of the universe for intelligent life, the remarkable specified complexity of the cell, or practically any other phenomena — physical, moral or conceptual — the arguments marshaled by theists have been almost exclusively intended to motivate monotheism.

Polytheism, which once held the place of prominence in natural theology, has thus been sorely neglected. On the one hand, this kindles an eagerness for a renaissance in polytheist philosophy. On the other hand, however, there is urgency for caution, as conclusions may only be seen to be premature after the discussion has developed.

Bearing this in mind, a natural theology is still a very important component of a theist's philosophical worldview, others include a developed opinion on what morality concerns, the nature of the mind and what knowledge consists in. As fascinating as it would be to construct (or at least defend) distinctively polytheist positions in these and related fields, I must reserve our attention for natural theology in this project.

It will not particularly matter whether the polytheist is Christian, Jewish or Pagan, the philosophical foundation I intend to lay will be able to support many different forms of polytheism. However, in the interests of full disclosure, I should let the reader know that I am a pagan, and will try to keep my biases in check.

In claiming that this natural theology is a philosophical foundation, I do not mean to comment on what role arguments ought to play in belief formation. Perhaps the appropriate (or even exclusive) means of attaining deeply seated belief in the gods is experience rather than reasoning. Whatever the case, the question before us is what reasons there are to believe that gods exist, not what role reasons ought to play in discerning whether gods exist.

My hope is that this work will help inspire thoughtful individuals to discuss and reevaluate the merits or demerits of polytheism.

Godhood

Let's begin by developing a working understanding of what gods might be like. With that in hand, we can then turn to discussing whether any gods exist, and if so, how many.

Fortunately, we don't have to start from scratch as if the concept of a god had never even crossed someone's mind before. On the contrary, we have handfuls of paradigmatic examples to draw from. However, these examples can differ to such an extent that it is difficult to find the common denominator between them that explains why they are gods instead of something else. For example, some might be completely disembodied, others composed of rock or sea, some remarkably benevolent, and others just downright nasty.

But our inability to uncover the individually necessary and jointly sufficient conditions of godhood is nothing to call home over. Like any other cluster of concepts correlated through a family resemblance, we only need a description that is recognizable as that of a god. For example, one way to tell whether something should count as a god or not is to compare it with our paradigmatic examples of deities. If it resembles them in the sense and to the extent that they resemble each other as gods, we should recognize it as a god.

But I want to take an easier — though no less effective — route. By using a selection of our paradigmatic examples of gods, I propose the following three conditions as sufficient for godhood:

(i):   Disembodied consciousness

(ii): Immensely more powerful than evolved minds

(iii): Remarkable greatness

Let's unpack each in turn.

Disembodied Consciousness

I wouldn't dare be so bold as to try and define what a conscious mind is. Given how little we know about it, the chances of my statements about the mind being true are proportional to their humility. But what I can do is describe my experience of the conscious mind and this will at least provide us with a basis for analogy.

Describing the experience of consciousness is not without its challenges though, as we quickly run out of words that are capable of breaking it down into more comprehensible notions: it's a very basic concept. Be that as it may, I feel my experience of it is best described as that of awareness. Sometimes it's an awareness of actions, other times of objects and their properties, and at other moments of events and situations.

Our awareness is largely mediated by senses. Taste, touch, hearing, sight and smell, all of which are ways we can become aware of things. But a disembodied consciousness would not have these, at least essentially — although it might be able to incarnate and take them on. This stirs trouble in the minds of some, and they fairly ask how such a thing is possible. You can't just...be aware of an object's dimensions or scent can you? Something must mediate that information to you. If, whilst sitting at my desk, I genuinely heard a dog barking it would be because the air-vibrations striking my eardrum have transmitted that information to me. Without any of these senses, what mediates the information of things — such as spatial dimensions, color or scent — to one's awareness? And what is awareness if you're not aware of anything?

Well, it is a very widely accepted view that consciousness does not entail intentionality. Intentionality is the property mental states — such as beliefs, thoughts or desires — typically have of being *about* something. When we believe, we believe something. When we think, we think about something. Our mental states are usually aimed at or directed toward things. However, through meditative techniques we are able to achieve a thoughtless awareness.[4] So, that consciousness is able to persist in the absence of intentionality is testable and verified. But how can intentional consciousness exist without the senses? That is, how can we be aware of things without our senses informing us of them? The information concerning what the object is like must get to us somehow if we're to be aware of it.

Let me begin by responding with a caveat: to argue that there are no senses available to a disembodied mind because we are ignorant of them is to commit the fallacy of *argumentum ad ignorantiam*. So, we must be very careful with what we are inferring here. Secondly, it is precisely because of our ignorance that we are unable to say with any confidence that disembodied conscious minds would have no way of receiving information about things, for they would only lack the physical mediators we're aware of, or are used to at any rate. Perhaps such minds would intuit things, in the same way that we intuit that nothing is taller or older than itself, for example.[5] This information, which is true of all things that exist, certainly didn't filter in through our retinas! We may not know how intuition works, but that it *does* seems reasonable. Thus, we are not really in a position to say it is unlikely that disembodied minds would acquire information by intuition. Perhaps our experience of proprioception can function as an analogue of what such awareness would be like. Finally, it seems the consensus that what most human beings have formed on this subject must count for something. The overwhelming majority of human beings have been either theists — who affirm the existence of numerous disembodied minds (including gods, angels, and even souls) — or atheists, who deny the existence of such disembodied minds. But in affirming or denying such things, we're acknowledging their coherence. If the concept of an intentional disembodied mind were unintelligible, it couldn't be true or false. And an implication of the principle of charity, which we've learned anew from Condorcet's Jury theorem, is that a consensus does not create truth: truth creates a consensus.

Many of our paradigmatic examples of deities would have disembodied consciousness: God is conceived of as being immaterial in the Bahá'í faith.[6]

> Traditional forms of Judaism, Christianity, and Islam each conceive of God as an immaterial, nonphysical reality... Because of the shared conviction that God is immaterial, Christians along with Jews and Muslims have historically opposed material conceptions of God or gods such as one finds in Stoicism, according to which God is a vast material being, a world soul or animal, and in polytheism, according to which there are hosts of material deities.[7]

As Taliaferro remarks, polytheism has traditionally been committed to the existence of material deities, though not exclusively. Many ancient traditions would assign divine status to material bodies like the Earth, sky, sun, mountains or rivers. In fact, numerous people maintain these traditions with a certain understanding of the so-called 'Gaia hypothesis'. Taliaferro means that polytheism affirmed hosts of essentially material deities since Christianity is not opposed to deities taking on material forms (Cf. Jesus' incarnation). But keep in mind that I'm not proposing disembodied consciousness as a necessary condition of godhood.

Immensely More Powerful than Evolved Minds

This property is deduced from the former. Consider that in common experience, I am able to move my hand just by willing it. But we don't ordinarily have this control over other material bodies: if I will to move your hand, I have to perform intermediate actions such as directing it with mine. Our actions are severely limited by our physical bodies. I cannot cross any distance without performing dozens of intermediate actions, and I am unable to acquire information, such as what something looks like, without utilizing the proper physical medium, even then retaining it only as long as the coffee I have digested permits me.

I take it that we should expect all evolved minds to have physical bodies. An evolved mind is just a consciousness that arises as a result of evolutionary processes. Un-embodied minds would be above the fray of such processes, as they only operate on material bodies. Liberated from such chains, these minds would be much more capable than embodied minds, making them superior in what they can apprehend, retain and achieve.

Granted, the phrase 'immensely more powerful' is ambiguous. But it is easier to recognize the immensity of this power than it is to define it. I do not think the cases of this power that we shall be considering will be vulnerable to this ambiguity.

Remarkable Greatness

Unfortunately, I have found it challenging to state just what exactly greatness is; but it seems to be that which is deserving of our awe. When you stand before a truly magnificent accomplishment, dwarfed in the shadow of a great pyramid for example, you might be struck by a sense of awe. It is reverence we feel, and we're impressed by it.

I recall being overcome by this impression when I visited Crazy Horse in the Black Hills, South Dakota. Its original sculptor — a Polish immigrant by the name of Korczak Ziolkowski — began this monumental tribute with only a couple hundred dollars in his pocket. But after pouring his soul into that mountain, he left behind something truly worthy of our respect.

It is important to describe greatness as that which deserves our awe instead of as that which happens to elicit our awe, because our awe may be elicited by something that is not great. For example, your *sensus magnae* (sense of greatness) would be malfunctioning if a team of wayward neuroscientists manipulated you to feel awe whenever you had to use the restroom. To deserve our awe is to be worthy of it.

With this initial understanding of greatness in hand, what do I mean by 'remarkable'? Well, I do not wish to claim that the greatness of these gods would be unsurpassed or unsurpassable, for I know of no good reason to think so. But it seems to me their greatness should be befitting of the greatest of gods. Perhaps this would be located in their extraordinary power, or unparalleled knowledge. Whatever the case, they would be as the Olympian gods were, compared to lesser deities.

Religions have time and again sacralized a subset of deities, setting them apart from everything else, recognizing in them a remarkable greatness.

> Being immortal, they were next, as a consequence supposed to be omnipotent and omniscient. Their physical strength was extraordinary, the earth shaking sometimes under their tread. Whatever they did was done speedily. They moved through space almost without the loss of a moment of time. They knew all things, saw and heard all things with rare exceptions. They were wise, and communicated their wisdom to men. They had a most strict sense of justice, punished crime vigorously, and rewarded noble actions...[8]

> In all mythologies the principal actors in the drama of cosmic creation begin as spirit beings so fundamental or so awe-inspiring, or both, as to be describable only as generalities.[9]

Ps. 77:13, Your way, O God, is holy; What god is great like our God?

Ex. 15:11, Who among the gods is like you, O LORD? Who is like you — majestic in holiness, awesome in glory, working wonders?

Ps. 86:8, Among the gods there is none like you, O Lord; no deeds can compare with yours.

Allah is called 'Lord of the worlds' (Surah 1:1:2), and none are like him. Further, the Qu'ran ascribes 99 names to Allah, and these make it abundantly clear that Allah is thought to stand at the height of greatness. Finally, Muslims praise Allah as the 'greatest' whenever they utter the Takbir, or the phrase Allahu Akbar (idiomatically meaning Allah is the greatest), which is recited in numerous contexts throughout their lives including their obligatory prayers and the adhan initiating them. Their greatness would be unmistakable!

I hope the foregoing has painted a recognizable image in our minds, one that we could feel comfortable with identifying as a god. It was derived from our paradigmatic examples of gods, after all. Obviously, gods would have innumerable other properties, but we're looking for something basic to begin with.

Now, one might object to the foregoing thought by raising various counter-examples. For example, a Christian, Jewish or Muslim theist might ask whether angels and demons satisfy our stipulated condition of godhood. If they do, perhaps such theists have good reason to believe our condition is insufficient for godhood, as entities could meet the condition but still fail to be gods. However, I ask the reader to take any particular angel or demon in mind and imagine that we had not learned of them through the sources we have, but that they had instead appeared within ancient pantheons, worshiped as gods. They would no longer be candidates for counter-examples, would they? Likewise, if we take a given deity and imagine we had instead learned of it through, say, an Abrahamic faith, which depicted it merely as an angel or demon, it would not be included in our paradigmatic examples of deities. What this tells us is that what might differentiate angels and demons from gods is not a matter of ontology, but of something else, perhaps even something so semantic and simple as the job they perform. After all, 'angel' does mean messenger, and polytheists believed in messenger gods — Hermes and Iris, for example.

Again, perhaps a Christian might raise the Trinity as a counter-example: 'each person of the Divine Trinity satisfies your condition, and yet it is not the case that each is a god, for they are all equally God. Therefore, your condition is insufficient'. But we should not have to accommodate every single example of a deity, only those which are paradigmatic, and given the bewildering amount of conflicting theories about the Christian Trinity, it is far from clear which is paradigmatic.

For example, the great Christian theologian Thomas Aquinas argued that because God is 'divinely simple', that is, without composition of any sort whatsoever, each aspect of the Trinity just had to be the different relations in God. Thus, the relation of paternity or 'being father of' is the person Christians refer to as the Father; and the relation of filiation or 'being son of' is the person Christians refer to as Jesus.[10] Despite being the star theologian of the demographically largest Christian denomination, this theory is mostly rejected by most Christian believers nowadays, if only because so few would affirm Divine Simplicity. However, the doctrine of Divine Simplicity has held considerable sway in Christian theology over the centuries:

[I]t must be admitted that a number of post-Nicene creeds, probably under the influence of the doctrine of divine simplicity, do include statements that can be construed to identify each person of the Trinity with God as a whole. For example, the Eleventh Council of Toledo (675) affirms, 'Each single person is wholly God in Himself', the so-called Athanasian Creed (fifth century) enjoins Christians 'to acknowledge every Person by himself to be God and Lord', and the Fourth Lateran Council, in condemning the idea of a divine Quaternity, declared, 'each of the Persons is that reality, viz., that divine substance, essence, or nature...what the Father is, this very same reality is also the Son, this the Holy Spirit'.[11]

Finally, we might just stand these objections on their heads and say it is precisely because angels, demons and the persons of the Trinity satisfy our condition of godhood that we have good reason to think that they are (or would be) gods.

Having identified a subset of gods for later discussion, what sorts of positions could we take on the existence of deities in general? We could either say that at least one god exists, that no gods whatsoever exist, that more than one god exists, or that only one god exists. It does not particularly matter what we call these sets of mutually exclusives, but let's label them for the sake of clarity and convenience. 'Theism' will be the position that at least one god exists, 'atheism' that no gods whatsoever exist, 'polytheism' that more than one god exists and 'monotheism' that no more than one god exists.

Given how controversial definitions of these terms can be, allow me to briefly defend my use of them. The idea here is that it is problematic to define these positions in terms of single or select deities. Far too often does theism refer to the position that God exists. Then what are we to call someone who believes in a god other than God? Are they not theists? Of course they are! Defining theism so narrowly renders its negation — atheism — horrendously implausible: not everyone who disbelieves in God is an atheist; they could be theists via their belief in a multitude of other gods. But they would have to be 'atheists' if theism was defined in terms of God. And so forth, for any other specific or select deity theism gets defined in terms of. For example, if I were to define 'god' in terms of the three-fold sufficient condition outlined above, I would immediately be confronted with the problem of those who believe in embodied gods, or gods of lesser greatness.

Furthermore, because of how narrowly these positions have been defined, it has caused unfortunate overconfidence in certain arguments. For example, problems of evil directed against God can be taken to establish that atheism is true, when at best they would only disconfirm single or select deities. To open the flood-gates and understand theism and atheism in as general a manner as we can goes a long way toward avoiding these problems, allowing us to speak about whether any deities exist, which is really where we should be starting anyway.

Let's turn now to whether there are any reasons to believe in a god.

Chapter 2

Is There a God?

Stumbling Blocks

Now that we have an idea of what a god might be like, is it even worth looking into whether any exist? Perhaps it seems, in advance of such considerations, that their existence is just too unrealistic.

Some of the most common reasons for dismissing the existence of gods include their apparent absence from our experience, and the purported improbability of disembodied minds. I will briefly interact with these objections to clear the way for the arguments in the next section. Harboring doubts like these could make one unreceptive to a case for theism, as we not only tend to apply stricter burdens of proof to positions we disagree with, but because it is difficult to truly appreciate the merits of an argument whose unsoundness seems like a foregone conclusion.

To the first question then, why aren't gods present in our experience? It may strike one as rather convenient that these gods exist, but that no one can see them. The most direct answer I have to this is that it is simply false: people have and do experience gods. But I must postpone a discussion into that until chapter three. For now, let us consider whether it is reasonable for us to expect gods to appear in our experience. If it is not, then there is simply no bite to this objection.

Why might a god appear to us? You may think a god would want to alleviate suffering, impart wisdom or even demand worship from us. However, each of these suggestions presupposes an awareness of what a god would be motivated to do. Without knowing any of her character traits, it would not be reasonable for us to expect a god to do anything in particular, much less alleviate suffering. Perhaps that is just the sort of thing she is disinclined to do! Imagine talking about some generic human being. We're hardly capable of predicting this person's behavior on the basis of their being human! We would need more information. While we may be able to deduce character traits from deities such as God (who is generally thought of as being perfect), we are not able to do so from the unspecified gods I have outlined above, for our sufficient condition of godhood contains no reference at all to moral natures. What about their greatness? Surely, this communicates some information about their inclinations?

Greatness can be located in any number of features, such as knowledge or power. So goodness is not the only progenitor of greatness. As such, we cannot know in advance whether these gods would be at all interested in interacting with people and in a state of such ignorance, it is not reasonable for us to expect them to appear in our experience.

One might concede this but maintain that disembodied minds are unrealistic: minds are unlikely to be disembodied because minds are likely to have brains. The trouble here is that this claim enjoys almost no inductive support. One could point to our knowledge gleaned from neuroscience, psychology or even our common experience of minds, and note the intimate ties they have with brains. But that is something we should expect of all evolved minds, *viz.* any mind arising as a result of evolutionary processes. Evolutionary processes favored this physical organ through thousands of variation and selection events because it has proven so excellent for survival and prosperity across challenging environments: of course evolved minds would have brains, or something like them. But why would non-evolved minds have brains? We expect certain minds to have brains because of evolutionary processes, processes that non-evolved minds would be uninfluenced by.

I'm suggesting that a mind is far more likely to have a brain given that it's a product of evolution than simply because it's a mind. There could be non-evolved minds, and there is no reason to expect them to have brains.

The thesis that there are no non-evolved minds is not supported by the cognitive sciences. They study evolved minds and their properties. At most, these fields suggest that evolved minds are unlikely to survive brain death and thus in a disembodied state (a largely defeasible conclusion).

Finally, seeing as the phrase 'non-evolved mind' communicates no information as to likely intentions or inclinations, we have no reason at all to expect to have observed such minds. Thus, any failure to have done so will surely not count against their existence. We are simply not in a position to say they are unlikely.

Theism

As I stated earlier, my purpose is to construct (or at least defend) a polytheist natural theology. But polytheism presupposes theism: the prefix 'poly', like 'mono', or 'a', quantitatively modifies theism. Since it is prudent to ensure that a foundation is stable before building on it, we will seek to verify the credentials of theism before investigating polytheism. Fortunately, monotheist and polytheist natural theologies will overlap with one another when it comes to defending theism. Thus, polytheists are able to tap into the valuable research of monotheist philosophers who erect cases for theism, and vice versa.

As the arguments for theism are far too many to even describe in a single chapter much less defend, I will have to be selective as to which I choose. I have decided to employ a cosmological argument not only because it seems to be sound, but because I think many atheists will find its premises plausible.

Note that because my conditions of godhood contain no reference to moral characters, considerations such as the evidential problems of evil, divine hiddenness or even the Euthyphro Dilemma are entirely irrelevant to my case. However, I do confront such problems in chapter four.

I have chosen to present my argument in a slightly formalized manner. This way, the reader can clearly see which claims I am making and which I am not. My assumptions and underlying logic will be laid bare for you to examine. This also has the advantage of keeping objections on track, as it is easy to simply ask 'exactly which premise is that objection aimed at?'.

I am going to assume that the reader has a basic under-standing of logic, however nothing in my argument requires one to know much of it.

An Argument for Theism

1. The existence of the universe is either due to its own necessary nature or to an external cause.
2. If it is due to an external cause, then at least one god exists.
3. The existence of the universe is not due to its own necessary nature.
4. Therefore, it is due to an external cause. (From 1 and 3.)
5. Hence, at least one god exists. (From 2 and 4.)

Explanation and Defense

The argument is logically valid, meaning if its premises [(1)-(3)] are true, then its conclusions [(4)-(5)] have to be true: they follow by the rules of logic. Thus, the most important thing to figure out when evaluating this argument is whether its premises are true.

By the universe I mean the entire space-time manifold. It does not particularly matter what shape this manifold takes: it may have an initial state, or it may extend infinitely into the past. In either case, the argument is concerned with why the manifold exists at all, and not with the existence of any of its regions in particular. This contrasts with other cosmological arguments, which focus instead on the universe's purported initial state. Some will no doubt object that 'the universe' is not a substance, but an aggregate of sorts. I ask such readers to understand 'the universe' to be a *façon de parler*, or a device of convenience for talking about each and every constituent of space-time at once. This is known as a 'fusion' in mereology, the science of parts and wholes:

> ...given a prior commitment to cats, say, a commitment to cat-fusions is not a further commitment. The fusion is nothing over and above the cats that compose it. It just is them. They just are it. Take them together or take them separately, the cats are the same portion of Reality either way. Commit yourself to their existence all together or one at a time, it's the same commitment either way. If you draw up an inventory of Reality according to your scheme of things, it would be double counting to list the cats and then also list their fusion. In general if you are already committed to some things, you incur no further commitment when you affirm the existence of their fusion.[1]

Finally, how could anything be external to the universe? Isn't the very notion of externality a spatial notion? I use 'external' simply to preempt talk of self-causation. Thus, a cause is external to its effect if it is distinct from it. Let's turn now to the premises, and see how plausible they are.

Premise (1): The existence of the universe is due either to its own necessary nature, or to an external cause.
The universe either causally depends on something in order to exist, or it does not. If it does, then the existence of the universe is due to whatever cause it depends upon. Since the universe would already need to exist in order to depend on itself for its existence, this cause would have to be external.

If, on the other hand, the universe does not causally depend upon anything in order to exist, then nothing could possibly make the universe stop existing, for if anything could, the universe would depend upon that not happening. Thus, if the universe does not causally depend on anything in order to exist, its existence is due to its own necessary nature. Therefore, the existence of the universe is due either to its own necessary nature, or to an external cause, just as premise (1) affirms.

Premise (2): If it is due to an external cause, then at least one god exists.

Being external to the universe, this cause would be non-physical (or disembodied). Being the cause of the universe, it would be terrifyingly great. And in virtue of being non-physical and the cause of the universe, it would be immensely more powerful than evolved minds. If this cause were a mind, it would thereby satisfy our sufficient condition of godhood. So, the question becomes, is it a mind?

Allow me to begin answering this question by outlining some background metaphysics that make an affirmative answer almost inevitable.

Consider that the universe is composed of different forms of matter: liquid, gaseous, solid, organic, inorganic, atomic, sub-atomic and so on and so forth. Matter can therefore take on a great variety of forms, some more substantial than others. Thus, melting a rubber ball into a puddle of goo involves the ball's matter (*viz.* rubber) changing forms in a much more substantial way than, say, merely changing color. A ball can go from red to green and still remain a ball, but it cannot survive being melted into goo.

A material substance will be composed of at least two features then: matter and form. It could not just be matter, for matter that is not in any form is not anything. But neither could it just be its substantial form, viz. the form which, when unified to matter, makes it whatever it essentially is, for then it wouldn't be a material substance. Material substances are thus constituted by their form and matter.

As Edward Feser illustrates, a red, rubber ball 'is composed of a certain kind of matter (namely rubber) and a certain kind of form (namely the form of a red, round, bouncy object). The matter by itself isn't the ball, for the rubber could take on the form of a doorstop, an eraser, or any number of things. The form by itself isn't the ball either, for you can't bounce redness, roundness, or even bounciness down the hallway, these being mere abstractions. It is only the form and matter together that constitute the ball'.[2]

It should be clear from the foregoing analysis that the claim 'matter is all that exists' is just nonsense: there simply cannot exist matter without any form. But can there be form without matter? Certainly, many well-respected thinkers have and continue to consider things such as minds, propositions and moral values to be immaterial. I neither want to beg the question against them, nor against those who suggest that the only forms that exist are those that are essentially conjoined to matter. In an attempt at neutrality then, I will say the following: most forms familiar to us are such that it is a necessary condition of their existence to be unified with matter. For example, if there were no matter, there could be no color, for it is of the essence of color to be conjoined with some matter or other (such as light-waves).

Considered apart from their matter, these forms are just abstractions in the mind, just concepts or ideas, for they only exist in reality in so far as they are united with matter. Given that these forms are just abstractions when considered apart from their matter, they are not 'contained' in matter, for the container and contained would have independent existence. As David Oderberg states, 'Hence the way in which essence is in substance is distinct from any sort of physical containment, since the relation between form and matter is one of union, not containment'.[3] Incidentally, but interestingly, considerations such as these afford rather strong reason to believe in the immateriality of our own minds. For, if our minds were just matter, they would inevitably take on whatever forms existed in them: when form unites with matter, that parcel of matter must reflect its form. But when the form of triangularity exists in my mind, my mind does not become a triangle. Nor does it become a tree when its form exists in my mind. Thus, my mind cannot be matter.

With the metaphysical distinction between matter and form in hand, let's reflect on how the form of the universe would relate to the cause of the universe. In so far as there is a cause of the universe (call it X), it will have caused the universe to exist by uniting the form of the universe with matter. Since there is no matter outside of the universe (recall our definition of the universe), this creative act could not have involved the simple rearranging of already pre-existent matter but would be the very bringing of matter into existence!

Now, consider that if X had not been geared (or predisposed) toward unifying the form of the universe with matter prior to doing so, there'd be no sufficient reason for why X did in fact produce this effect rather than another. As Thomas Aquinas explained:

> Were an agent not to act for a definite effect, all effects would be indifferent to it. Now that which is indifferent to many effects does not produce one rather than another [lest it, in fact, be different to one]. Therefore, from that which is indifferent to either of two effects, no effect results, unless it be determined by something to one of them. Hence it would be impossible for it to act. Therefore, every agent tends toward some definite effect, which is called its end.[4]

If X hadn't been inclined (whether consciously or by nature) toward unifying the form of the universe with matter (instead of doing something else), this unification wouldn't really be due to X's activity, but would rather merely be coincident with it. It'd be dumb luck that this of all effects happened to obtain. But, in so far as X was geared toward making the form of the universe instantiate prior to doing so, the form of the universe must have existed in some sense prior to being instantiated. Otherwise, there would be nothing for X to be geared toward producing. However, as noted above, apart from their matter, such forms are just abstractions existing in the mind. Thus, given the existence of X, the form of the universe must not only have existed in a mind prior to the creation of the universe, but as the goal of X's activity. Therefore, in so far as there is a cause of the universe, it will ultimately be a mind.

In fact, given that it is matter which requires a substance to reflect whatever form it has, and that it is intellect which allows a substance to have forms other than its own, not only would the cause of the universe be a mind (as it has many forms other than its own), but its intellect would be unsurpassable as it would be the furthest thing from matter, and thus the least limited intellect.

Furthermore, what could this cause possibly be if it were not a mind? Everything encountered in our experience (scientific and otherwise) is either a mind, or something physical. And try as they might, our imaginations can only combine in new and strange ways what we have already encountered through experience. This makes it difficult to take the option seriously, for we are essentially committed to saying that x did y, and that made the universe. But such a claim is hardly informative. So, whatever problems arise from saying the cause is a mind, we must sincerely ask ourselves this: are they really as troublesome as those that arise from the cause being unintelligible?

Let us then move on and consider what else may be said in favor of this cause being a mind. For starters, there is really only one form of causation we are familiar with whereby something non-physical exerts causal influence over something physical, and that is mental causation.[5] Minds are somehow able to causally influence matter: it is how I have moved my fingers to type, and you your eyes to read. True, mental causation involving non-physical substances has become very controversial nowadays. But knowing that mental causation works, our ignorance as to how it does will not amount to saying that mental causation is unintelligible: at least we have a well-known category of causation here. And some objections to mental causation lose all force in this scenario. For example, it is sometimes objected that causal operations in nature can be completely understood in physical (or more generally, scientific) terms. The upshot is that mental causation is not only superfluous, but would seem to violate principles of conservation. But there are no natural causal operations to appeal to when discussing the cause of the universe. Thus, mental causation is neither superfluous nor would it violate principles of conservation.

Finally, because there would be no laws of nature prior to nature for science to appeal to, it is impossible to give a scientific explanation of this cause. But given that there is an external cause of the universe, there must be some explanation of it. So, what could such a non-scientific explanation be?

The only other type of explanation familiar to us is personal explanation. In a personal explanation, we explain the occurrence of an event via the intentions of an agent.[6] For example, imagine a family bustling along in a kitchen getting ready for the day. Suddenly, a chair is knocked over, making a loud crash. "Who did it?!" the mom hollers. "It was Billy!", one of the daughters responds. She has explained the crash in personal terms, rather than in scientific ones. We use this form of explanation practically every single day. It is presupposed by questions such as 'Who wrote that book?' and 'Who built the pyramids?'.

Thus, well-known categories of causation and explanation suggest that this cause is a mind. And in light of the absence of competitors, this is the best explanation available to us.

As stated above, the cause of the universe being a mind brings us to our threefold condition of godhood: this cause would be a remarkably great disembodied mind that is immensely more powerful than evolved minds.

Premise (3): The existence of the universe is not due to its own necessity.

Oftentimes, cosmological arguments discuss whether the universe is contingent or necessary. But our data seems too inconclusive to allow one position or the other to gain a decisive advantage.

For example, traditionally, those who argue that the universe is contingent suggest that if the universe were necessary, then our commonsense intuitions about possibilities would be illusory and there would be no free will. But this is to view all the states of the universe at once when discussing whether the universe is necessary or contingent. An alternative approach is to ask whether any part of the universe is necessary, for if any part were, then even if every contingent state of the universe ceased to exist, the universe would still have to exist by virtue of that part. In such a scenario, it is easy to conceive of us as living in contingent states of the universe, thus preserving our common-sense intuitions about possibilities and free will.

However, cosmological arguments need not be delayed by these stagnated discussions because, surprisingly, it makes no difference whether the universe is necessary or contingent...or so I claim. If the universe is contingent, then it does not have a necessary nature for its existence to be due to. And if it does have a necessary nature, then it received this from an external cause. How could the universe receive a necessary nature from an external cause? Well, imagine that a god created the universe, but that it could not have done otherwise. In such a case, the universe will have a necessary nature, but its existence will not be due to that nature: it will be due to the external cause that gave it that nature.

The universe would receive its necessary nature from an external cause because the universe is constituted by parts that don't just come conjoined: they need to be conjoined by an external cause, and the universe could not do this since it only exists once they've been conjoined. What are these parts, and why must something conjoin them? We have already been introduced to them: matter and form. Something must explain why two distinct things, *viz.*, a material object's form and its matter, are united together, and we can only say this something is one of three things:

(i): The form or its matter in isolation from the other
(ii): The form and its matter in conjunction with one another
(iii): Something other than the form and its matter

But (i) is impossible since neither these forms nor their matter exist apart from the other, and (ii) is impossible since cause logically precedes effect and the conjunction of a form with its matter cannot logically precede itself. Therefore, the only other option is (iii): what unites a form with its matter must be an external cause. Note also that this external cause must keep the form of a material substance united with its matter at every single moment of its existence, for at no point whatsoever can the union be explained by either (i) or (ii). Thus, the external cause of the universe is not some distant clockmaker, but intimately present at every single moment.

What all this means is that the universe is composed of parts, which cannot exist at any point whatsoever unless they are made to by an external cause. Now, this external cause may conjoin the universe's form with its matter in a necessary way, or in a contingent way. But, either way, the existence of the universe must be due to an external cause.

Conclusion

I have heard it said that philosophy is just science with less data. I won't pretend that my case for theism is rationally indisputable. Instead, my hope is to have presented a reasonable case for theism. My claim is not that reason requires acceptance of my arguments, but that it permits them: people may rationally dispute my arguments, but they may also rationally endorse them. This is often the best we can do in philosophy: until our data set increases, the variability of reasonable interpretations over that set will remain rather open ended. Yet, despite this, I believe the foregoing arguments to be good, and capable of being endorsed by skeptics and non-believers alike.

My case for polytheism should remain unimpeded for the theist reader who remains unconvinced by this argument, for presumably, she will have some other reason for believing in theism, and can proceed to the next chapter on that basis. However, before moving on, I invite the reader to briefly pause and contemplate how this argument might impact her worldview. Given that the premises are true, there must be a god. But, if there really is a god out there, and one who created the universe to boot (we'll explore whether she acted alone later on), how does this affect your view of things? The practical and theoretical implications can be exciting to think about. What are our prospects of contacting her? Could she help us discover cures to diseases? If she created a life-permitting universe, did she create an after-life as well? Why has she allowed me, out of all possible human beings, to breathe?

Chapter 3

How Many Gods Are There?

Tradition

Traditionally, arguments for monotheism have consisted in the attempt to show that no more than one perfect being can exist.[1] But this was either predicated on the assumption that in order to be a god, a being must be perfect, or on the assumption that the only god that exists is perfect. Yet the overwhelming majority of our paradigmatic examples of deities are of imperfect beings. As John Michael Greer explains: '[I]n traditional polytheism, gods are neither infinite, nor timeless, nor changeless. They are held to possess superhuman capacities of power and knowledge, but these powers aren't unlimited, and the gods themselves are subject to change like any other being'.[2] Moreover, it is simply question begging to assert that monotheism is true. In light of this, I take the issue to be semantic: these arguments were not really concerned with how many gods exist, but with how many *supreme* gods exist. However, since monotheism and polytheism are about how many gods exist (whether perfect or imperfect), I take these arguments to be irrelevant to my case for polytheism. If anything, their success merely adds weight to theism.

The Initial Perspective

Before moving on to consider arguments that are independent of those given in the previous chapter, let us see whether our conclusions can do any further philosophical work for us.

You'll recall that we concluded that the existence of the universe is due to at least one god. But is it due to just one god? Well, it either is or it isn't. In other words, one of the following propositions must be true:

1. Only one god caused the universe to exist.
2. More than one god caused the universe to exist.

Note how polytheism and monotheism relate to these propositions. Polytheism is compatible with either (1) or (2) being true since (1) merely says only one god caused the universe to exist, not that only god exists, and (2) entails polytheism. Monotheism, on the other hand, is only compatible with (1) since as noted, (2) requires polytheism.

Which proposition is most likely to be true? Well, the monotheist will say (1) and the polytheist may say either. But in constructing a natural theology, we cannot stand on foundations that have not yet been laid. Thus, until either position is argued for, we must approach this question simply as a theist.

So, what should a theist say? The problem is that if she favors any answer at this point — that is, prior to considering any evidence for or against polytheism, she will thereby take a stand on the state of our evidence for polytheism and monotheism. If she says that (1) is more likely than (2), she rejects the polytheist arguments for (2) which she hasn't yet considered. If she says that (2) is more likely than (1), she rejects monotheism, a conclusion she has no argument for. And if she says neither is more likely than the other, she not only rejects the polytheist arguments in favor of (2) but also the arguments for monotheism which entail that (2) is false and therefore that (1) is more likely. Her only available option is to say that she doesn't know which proposition, if either, is most likely.

Surprisingly, being in this state of ignorance gives her reason to adopt polytheism. Accepting that the existence of the universe is due to at least one god, she knows that one of these propositions has to be true: her deity was either the only god who created or it was not. Since polytheism could be true either way, but monotheism could not, polytheism has a higher chance of being true from her perspective. Therefore, the conclusion from the previous chapter is able to do some more philosophical work for us after all: we are able to infer that polytheism is more likely than monotheism. Note this is not to say a polytheistic creation is more likely than a monotheistic creation.

Now, one might worry that this result is only derivable from the argument of chapter two, or at least its conclusion. But, it can be replicated with nearly every theistic conclusion. Take the conclusion of a teleological argument for theism as representative. Let's word the conclusion as follows:

Teleological Conclusion: The fine-tuning of the initial conditions of the universe for life is due to at least one god.

But is it due to just one god? Well, it either is or it isn't. That is, we're faced with a familiar dilemma:

1. Only one god fine-tuned the initial conditions of the universe for life.
2. More than one god fine-tuned the initial conditions of the universe for life.

Once again, if the theist says (1) is more likely than (2), that (2) is more likely than (1), or that neither is more likely than the other, she takes a premature stand on the state of our evidence for polytheism or monotheism. Thus, she must abstain from commitment, and because polytheism is compatible with either (1) or (2) but monotheism is not, she must evaluate polytheism as having a higher chance of being true than monotheism.

This result is interesting for a couple of reasons. For starters, at this point the theist has good reason to believe in polytheism and no good reason to believe in monotheism. Thus, she can reasonably believe in polytheism. Moreover, she can maintain this belief even if she never finds another reason to believe in polytheism: her burden is met, and has shifted to monotheists. Perhaps this reason isn't good enough to warrant a highly confident belief in polytheism. But the theist may at least say things like this: 'I don't know that polytheism is true, but chances are it is'. Furthermore, and because of this, it significantly affects what standards we should hold the arguments in the next section to. On the one hand, when you encounter an argument against a position you hold (call it H), that argument must do more work than it has to for someone who doesn't accept H. This is because it not only has to convince you of its conclusion (as it does for someone who doesn't hold H) but it also has to overcome your confidence in H. On the other hand, when you encounter an argument in favor of H, that argument doesn't have to do as much work for you as it does for someone who rejects H.

Some would suggest that this confidence will be short lived because there are problems with the claim that a group of deities created the universe. For example, it has been argued that such a group would quarrel, producing a much more disordered universe than the one we observe. The Qur'an puts it like this:

> Allah has not taken any son, nor has there ever been with Him any deity. [If there had been], then each deity would have taken what it created, and some of them would have sought to overcome others. - Qur'an 23:91

> If there were numerous gods instead of one, [the heavens and the earth] would be in a sorry state. - Qur'an 21:22

John Damascus (a 'Doctor of the Church') argued similarly: 'Further, how could the world be governed by many and saved from dissolution and destruction, while strife is seen to rage between the rulers? For difference introduces strife.'[3]

We cannot know whether a group of gods would quarrel unless we had an idea about their characters and personalities, and at least as I have construed them, we do not. Moreover, why would the quarreling of immaterial substances result in physical effects? It is not as if gods can only harm each other through impact, or contact. Finally, if difference really did introduce strife, it would seem John's Trinitarian God would be in trouble.

Others may object that we have reason to prefer (1) to (2) because it's simpler. But, suppose that (1) is simpler than (2). It's even simpler than either of these to just say that the universe was created by at least one god: the monotheistic and polytheistic claims take this theistic position as a given, and add information to it by specifying just how many gods were involved. So if simplicity does confer preference, then we do not have reason to prefer (1) to (2), as the theistic hypothesis is even simpler. But is (1) simpler? In some respects sure, but not necessarily in all respects, and it's unclear which should matter. Obviously, (1) is numerically simpler since it posits fewer entities. But (2) could posit simpler entities as we would need to invest a single deity with enormous amounts of power and knowledge for it to account for the universe all on its own.

Bearing these considerations in mind, let us bid chapter two farewell and take a look at some other arguments for polytheism.

Religious Experience

I will argue that it is reasonable to trust what perceptual experiences of gods represent there to be, and that they represent there to be a multitude of deities. The result will be that our suspicion that polytheism is true gets empirically confirmed.

Perceptual experiences of gods (from now on just 'theistic perceptual experiences') are a species of perceptual experiences, and the reason I think we should trust the former is the same reason I think we should trust the latter. So, allow me to begin by analyzing the reliability of perceptual experiences in general.

There are three primary elements, which together constitute a genuine perception. The first is having a perceptual experience, which is a mental state that assertively represents there to be something external to the subject. For example, your mind is representing that there are words in front of you right now as if they were really there. That is, as if it were asserting they were there. Secondly, there must actually be something external to the subject, which is at least roughly as it is represented by the perceptual experience. You cannot genuinely be perceiving words if there are no such words external to your mind. Finally, the external object must be causing the perceptual experience. You may very well be having a perceptual experience of there being words before you, and there may even be such words on a page somewhere in the world, but unless they are causing your experience, by reflecting light, for example, it's just luck that your perceptual experience corresponds to what it represents there to be.

So, should we trust that things are as our perceptual experiences represent them to be? Why think there is an external object roughly satisfying our mental content, or that it is the object of our experience instead of something else which is causing the state?

One thing is clear: we should not (nor could we) rely exclusively on evidence in order to trust our perceptual experiences. If we had to have evidence for our perceptual experiences before we could reasonably trust them, we couldn't trust in the experiences we crucially depend upon. For example, we couldn't trust our perceptual experience that there is a world external to our minds. Sure, it seems to us that there is a world external to our minds. But we can't argue for a real world outside of our minds without appealing to our experiences of it, which is circular. Thus, the only way we can reasonably hold this belief is if its justification doesn't depend upon or derive from evidence, but instead just comes justified by default. Furthermore, since practically all of our other beliefs about history, physics, biology, politics, and even our memories presuppose that there is a real world outside our heads, it is literally our rationality itself that hangs in the balance. And this holds for perceptual experiences in general, not just those of the external world. If we were unable to reasonably accord our perceptual experiences a default trust in the absence of defeating considerations, we would be trapped in an uncompromising skepticism. Our only means of coming to reasonably trust a perceptual experience would be to verify its content. But we could only verify its content by having other perceptual experiences! And we would meet each perceptual experience with doubt, thus left unable to verify any of them. We need self-authentication.

As such, it is a non-negotiable principle of rationality that we may reasonably trust our perceptual experiences unless and until we have good reasons not to. Note that this principle is not limited to certain kinds of perceptual experiences, such as those of material objects. This principle has gone by various titles including 'The Principle of Credulity' and the 'Principle of Phenomenal Conservatism'.[4,5] I will continue the tradition of referring to it as the former. With this principle in mind, we have a fairly straightforward argument for polytheism.

An Argument for Polytheism

1.   If gods have been perceived, then polytheism is true.
2.   Gods have been perceived.
3.   Therefore, polytheism is true.

Explanation and Defense

This simple and straightforward argument is logically valid. As is customary then, we'll focus on appraising its premises. Fortunately, there are only two of them.

Premise (1): If gods have been perceived, then polytheism is true.

Recall that a perception is a perceptual experience that is caused by the object it represents there to be. Thus, a god is perceived just in case there is a god that causes someone to have a perceptual experience of it. As such, if more than one god has been perceived, then there is more than one god, as they have caused people to have perceptual experiences of them. And the existence of more than one god is precisely what polytheism declares. I take it that this premise is indisputable.

Premise (2): Gods have been perceived.

I argued above that it is reasonable to trust a perceptual experience unless and until we have good reason not to. It follows that if people have had perceptual experiences of gods, then it is reasonable to trust those experiences unless and until we have good reason not to. My first goal then is to show that people have indeed had perceptual experiences of gods. For many of us, this will be all that is needed to show that premise (2) is true, for we lack good reasons to doubt these perceptual experiences (even if we find them hard to believe, a sensation that does not actually constitute an objection). However, some do take themselves to have good objections to these perceptual experiences, and therefore, I will turn to those next and investigate whether any are successful.

So then, has it ever actually seemed to anyone that a deity was present? Well, one thing is for sure — many, many people have claimed as much:

> The experience included a sublime consciousness of a person- alized sustaining power which defies description. I recall wondering whether I had found God or had God found me. I was infinitely more concerned with and aware of people and my environment. Mental perception and originality of thought were heightened. Living reached undreamed of levels of sheer joy....I was at first surprised to discover little corre- lation between my experience and the Church's beliefs and behavior.[6]

But the more I seek words to express this intimate inter-course, the more I feel the impossibility of describing the thing by any of our usual images. At bottom the expression most apt to render what I felt is this: God was present, though invisible, he fell under no one of my senses, yet my consciousness perceived him.[7]

Dr. Eben Alexander has recently published the book *Proof of Heaven*.[8] The book is essentially his medical analysis — as a professional neurosurgeon — of an experience he had while his neo-cortex was inoperative for about a week. During his 'Near Death Experience', Dr. Alexander took himself to perceive a god whom he calls 'Aum' (because of the sound it seemed to generate). It is then quite uncontroversial that people have claimed to perceive deities.

Now the question arises, is there any good reason to doubt that these people have really had these perceptual experiences?

I submit that it is reasonable to trust that things are as others report them to be unless and until we have good reason not to. Almost all of our knowledge is based on this sort of trust. For instance, I haven't the time or ability to check the historical claims of my chemistry text book (by repeating experiments and so forth). I just have to trust. I similarly trust testimonials from news reporters as well as memories of what gas prices used to be like, or humorous childhood anecdotes. When the weather man tells me how likely it is to rain, I trust. Reflecting a little on the amount of our knowledge that is based on the testimony of others reveals not only that we really should trust testimony in the absence of good defeaters, but that we don't trust other's testimony because of their credentials (how many of our family members who have taught us so much lack university degrees altogether?).

The German philosopher Immanuel Kant observed something very interesting about language. Why do you think lying works? Isn't that a strange phenomenon? We're able to lie to others, or deceive them into thinking that something false is actually true because we're expected to tell the truth! If everyone (or most people) lied, we wouldn't trust each other and lying wouldn't work. I don't feel, therefore, that I'm asking anyone to embrace a fringe epistemic practice: initially trusting others is the status quo.

In contrast to the view that beliefs based on testimony are inferential, renowned epistemologist Robert Audi says this:

> [B]eliefs about the credibility of the attester and beliefs pertinent to the attested proposition play a mainly filtering role: they prevent our believing testimony that does not 'pass', for instance because it seems insincere; but if no such difficulty strikes us, we 'just believe' (non-inferentially) what is attested. These filtering beliefs are like a trap door that shuts only if triggered. Its normal position is open, but it stays in readiness to block what should not enter. The open position is a kind of trust.[9]

The foregoing is intended to show that we should trust the claim that people have had perceptual experiences of deities unless and until we have good reason not to. In other words, the claim under investigation should be regarded as innocent until proven guilty. Such trust is normal and reasonable. No doubt, some folks will make claims like these for attention, credibility, or out of confusion and so forth. But given that most of us have not even heard the majority of such testimonials, we are hardly in a position to judge them as so problematic.

As noted above, for many of us, the foregoing will be all that is needed to justify premise (2). Once those of us who have no good reason to reject all perceptual experiences of gods as unreliable admit that people have had such experiences, we're committed to the accuracy of such experiences. I invite the reader to truly reflect on whether she has good reasons to think that all perceptual experiences of gods are unreliable. What could give someone such an insight into these experiences? As I hope to show next, there are no such considerations.

We'll begin with a family of arguments that suggest that theistic perceptual experiences are not actually perceptual!

Perceptual Objections

Generally, in arguing that theistic perceptual experiences are not even perceptual, the interlocutor will attempt to identify some condition that an experience must meet if it is to be perceptual, and argue that experiences of gods fail to meet it.

As far as I know, there are no conditions of perceptual experiences known to us *a priori* that purportedly theistic perceptual experiences fail to meet. For example, they are in principle falsifiable since, for instance, establishing that no gods exist would defeat them. And it is not a condition of perceptual experiences that they be capable of intersubjective verification, for that applies only to public objects (things which are by and large visible to our senses, like rocks and trees), not to private objects (things which are by and large invisible to our senses, like sensations, memories or gods as the case may be).

Still, one might furnish an *a posteriori* objection perhaps by inferring from some sample of perceptual experiences that all perceptual experiences meet a condition which theistic experiences uniformly fail to. The sample is almost always perceptual sensorial experiences, such as of seeing trees, hearing music, or tasting coffee. The problem with this sort of objection, as I see it, is that for every proposed condition, it is unclear why it's not just a condition for some smaller class of experiences to be perceptual instead of all experiences in general.

For instance, Herman Philipse has argued that since sense-perceptions are the experiences standardly justified by the principle of credulity, unless a theistic experience sufficiently resembles sense-perception, the principle should be restricted from it.[10] But why must theistic experiences sufficiently resemble sense-perceptions rather than just perceptual experiences in general? Is it because Dr. Philipse has implicitly identified the set of sense-perceptions with the set of perceptual experiences in general? If so, he has simply begged the question. He might deny this and say he was instead relying on sense-perceptions as a guide since they're far less controversial than non-sensorial-perceptions. But, even using them as guides is problematic because sense-perceptions differ from one another so dramatically that it's not only unclear why this set of diverse experiences should be the paradigms of perceptual experience, but which of their features should count as paradigmatic.

We learn what we can have perceptual experience of, by having perceptual experiences. Recall that people have explicitly said they were having such experiences of some deity or other. To object that they were not is to accuse them of some sort of incompetence or ulterior motive, as if they did not know what it's like to have a perceptual experience or were lying. However, I'm guessing that most of us are not in a position to know these sorts of things about those who claim to have had perceptual experiences of deities. It seems to me then that the reasonable thing to do is to simply trust that they genuinely had experiences in which their minds represented there to be some god or other.

Let's consider another sort of objection. While accepting that there are perceptual experiences of gods, this next set of arguments more or less suggest that there is something about them which prevents them from being accurate. We'll call these the prevention objections for simplicity.

Prevention Objections

Let's reflect a little deeper on what might prevent a perceptual experience from being accurate. What are some examples of things that would depreciate the accuracy of a perceptual experience?

Well, if after struggling through a hot desert for days without adequate water, food or sleep, an individual takes herself to be perceiving a large body of clear, cool water...we're inclined to write the experience off as a mirage due to malnutrition, dehydration or sleep-deprivation. Likewise, when someone takes herself to perceive a 50-foot tall giant after having consumed a generous amount of LSD, we are sooner to regard it as hallucinatory than accurate. With sense-perceptual experiences, we generally look for deviations in the normal course of experience, such as harmful ingestion, neurochemical imbalances or similar.

But it would seem foolish to think these more obvious defeaters, such as harmful ingestion, sleep deprivation or even minor temporal lobe seizures, were present in some combination or other for every single religious experience that has ever occurred, especially if one has not conducted the appropriate research into all the religious experiences out there. It would seem to be an irresponsible extrapolation from the few studies so far conducted to the thousands upon thousands of experiences out there. Ironically, testimonies often speak of the surprising nature of these experiences precisely *because* none of these defeating considerations were present!

The experience itself is very difficult to describe. It took me completely by surprise. I was about to start shaving at the time, of all things. I felt that my soul was literally physically shifted — for quite a number of seconds, perhaps 15 to 20 from the dark into the light. I saw my life, suddenly, as forming a pattern and felt that I had, suddenly, become acquainted with myself again...I must stress here that prior to this experience I never used to use the words such as 'soul' or 'salvation' or any such 'religiously coloured' words. But in order to make even the slightest sense of what happened to me I find it imperative to use them.[11]

Furthermore, given our arguments for theism, we are unable to say things like 'it's more likely that this person was stressed out, sleep-deprived, ingested mind-altering substances (etc., etc.) than that they really perceived a god'. Given the initial trust I've argued testimonies deserve, the burden is on the skeptic to find a good defeater. She must show that the person is a habitual liar, or could gain substantial wealth or fame from making the claim and so forth.

But I don't know these people, and I'm guessing the reader does not either. I have no reason to think they are making this up or suffering from some disorder. If you are anything like me, and I suspect most of us are in this boat together, let us just continue the normal epistemic practice of trusting others testimonies until we have good reason not to.

In a peculiar way, monotheism provides us with a prevention objection. Theistic perceptual experiences appear to be quite diverse in the gods they represent there to be. People have taken themselves to perceive everything from Shiva, Allah, or Cernunnos to Jesus of Nazareth surrounded by legions of angels. If there really was only one god, most of these experiences would be unreliable, since these experiences would by and large be representing there to be gods that did not technically exist. But this would mean theistic perceptual experiences are generally unreliable, usually taking things that don't exist as their objects, and therefore that the principle of credulity should not be applied to them. They would be guilty until shown innocent. Thus it would seem that if monotheism were true, the principle of credulity would have to be restricted from theistic perceptual experiences. Because monotheism precludes the existence of the numerous deities being 'perceived' in these experiences, Herman Philipse says:

It follows that all experiences (apparently) of God are indeed experiences (apparently) of 'an object of a certain kind in circumstances where similar perceptual claims have proved false', for God and other deities belong to the common kind of supernatural beings. So it seems that [mono]theists are landed in a dilemma at this point. Either they have to convert to polytheism and live with the swamp of gullibility or they have to abandon the argument from religious experience [12]

I'll come back to the swamp of gullibility remark shortly. So, this bears two interesting implications for our investigation. First, those who are more sure that the principle of credulity should apply to at least some theistic perceptual experiences than that monotheism is true have a good reason to reject monotheism. These folks could include individuals whose religious belief ultimately rests on theistic perceptual experiences: unless the principle of credulity applies, their religious belief crumbles. I doubt that most believers maintain theism on grounds other than such experiences. It also includes individuals who simply lack reason to believe monotheism, such as myself (I have never had a theistic perceptual experience). Second, for those who do hold monotheism (whether because of theistic perceptual experiences or not), they must weigh the relevant probabilities here. What is more likely, that only one god exists or that theistic perceptual experiences — like all other perceptual experiences — are innocent until shown guilty? I think members of the great faiths are faced with an interesting conundrum at this point.[13] Without the principle of credulity, how are they to trust — for example — the Apostle's alleged theistic perceptual experiences? How are they to trust any of the Old Testament prophet's experiences (without which, the reliability of the revelation they communicated may be compromised)?[14] In 1 Corinthians 15, St. Paul said that without Jesus' resurrection, Christian faith is useless and that Christians are to be the most pitied of all men. And without the Apostle's theistic perceptual experiences, there doesn't seem to be a case for the resurrection. The Christian apologist may wish to argue that she does not need the principle of credulity to reasonably believe in the Apostle's experiences, instead relying on things like inference to best explanation. But I doubt the apologist has evaluated her argument's strength in light of the unreliability of religious experiences that her inability to apply the principle of credulity to theistic perceptual experiences would require. If they sacrifice the principle of credulity at this point, it seems they will also lose their faith. But if they sacrifice their belief that no other gods exist but theirs, they need not give up these theistic perceptual experiences. Monolatrism, the belief in many gods but reservation of worship for only one, was an acceptable position within 2nd Temple Judaism and early Christianity.[15]

So, it would seem that in so far as monotheism provides a prevention objection and it is reasonable to apply the principle of credulity to theistic perceptual experiences, we have good reason to doubt monotheism.

Another example of a prevention objection goes something like this: since we can artificially reproduce theistic perceptual experiences we have more or less identified their proximate causes, thus, positing deities is explanatorily superfluous.

However, we can artificially reproduce visual experiences of trees as well. Does that mean visual experiences of trees are unreliable, or that positing real trees to explain these experiences is explanatorily superfluous? Of course not. So, just because an experience (or kind of experience) can be artificially reproduced does not mean that the experience (or its kind) is generally unreliable. To say that the brain-events which played a causal role in producing a theistic perceptual experience account for the causes of such an experience is like saying the brain-events which played a causal role in producing a visual experience of a tree account the causes of a visual experience of a tree. One would rightly note that many visual experiences of trees have...well...trees, and the light they reflect (etc.) as causes as well. But, one might say, we have reason to postulate the existence of trees and the light they reflect to explain these visual experiences, but no reason to postulate a deity to explain theistic perceptual experiences. However, as I have argued we do have good reason to posit gods...at least initially. We should accord trust to perceptual experiences unless and until we have good reason not to, not the other way around.

Furthermore, it should come as no surprise that the brain is involved in theistic perceptual experiences: it's involved in all of our other experiences. Some theists have tried to turn this objection on its head and argue that the parts of the brain which play a significant role in producing theistic perceptual experiences were designed by a deity to do as much. But we needn't go that far. It's not as if gods would have needed to design the brain, or they wouldn't know how to produce such perceptual experiences in us. We have practically no idea how our brain works, but that does not prevent our knowledge of how to get each other's attention.

Besides, as Evan Fales says:

A theist may wish to reply here that God may well have a hand in these mechanisms, indeed employ them as his means for appearing to his worshippers. But this is implausible on a number of counts. For one thing, it is extraordinarily hard to explain why God would appear through the figure of Jesus to a Christian, as Allah to a Muslim, Brahman to a Hindu, the god Flesh to a Dinka, and as a variety of Ioa spirits to voodoo practioners.[16]

Obviously, this problem does not befall polytheism. Next up, we have the infamous theory ladeness objection. Essentially, this states that perceptual experiences of deities are so heavily influenced by interpretation, the experience itself is unlikely to be much at all like its interpretation.

Graham Oppy has put this concisely:

> While it may not be true universally, it is clear that similar considerations apply to very many cases of revelation and selective ('private') religious experiences. Since these are so rarely reported by those who are not already religious believers – or by those who are not embedded in a community in which there is considerable religious fervour – there are good reasons for non-believers to suspect that there is pollution by prior theory in these cases as well.[17]

I should note before addressing this more directly that Dr. Eben Alexander was a staunch naturalist whose experience cannot plausibly be written off to prior theory pollution, and he is certainly not alone in this. In any case, I think Kai-Man Kwan has more than ably responded to this objection.[18] It's actually a composite claim: first, it alleges that an experient's prior theory has a heavy influence on the content of their theistic perceptual experience, and second that this influence tends to render the experience unreliable.

As Kwan says, there is no problem with the first allegation. It's commonly admitted by philosophers of science as well as psychologists that perceptions in general are theory laden (especially sense-perceptions).[19] There is no reason to exempt religious experiences from this. The problem is why this prior theory should render a perception unreliable. The mere presence of prior theory is certainly not debilitating because we know it can actually assist us. For example, if it weren't for prior theory, I would not be identifying the loud, flying metallic object as a jet or the yipping ball of fur as a dog. The point is that if it were just the mere presence of prior theory that rendered an experience unreliable, then all of our perceptual experiences would be unreliable.

The quintessential challenge that every detractor of the

arguments from religious experience must face is to identify a defeater that applies to theistic perceptual experiences, but not to other experiences. Otherwise, their objections will be self-refuting.

I should note the stock objection in passing that religious experiences are unreliable since they are contradictory. One person reports having seen God in purgatory, while the other has seen Allah. But, if Allah exists...purgatory does not and vice versa. At best, this objection should compel us to dismiss those perceptual experiences that do in fact contradict each other, not refute *all* theistic perceptual experiences whatsoever. Further, it's not at all clear that theistic perceptual experiences are actually what are contradicting each other. On the contrary, religious experiences sometimes contradict religious beliefs, but there is nothing at all contradictory about the co-existence of Allah and YHWH: only the associated beliefs that the one or the other is the only god that exists. I see no reason why we should not derive our religious beliefs from theistic perceptual experiences. If we treated these experiences as Christians treat the Bible (that is, as an authoritative source to guide the contents of religious belief), we would come up with a consistent, albeit novel theology. For example, there would be multiple after-lives for different people, etc.

Sometimes, monotheists will concede that theistic perceptual experiences are at their roots reliable, but attempt to explain away the apparent diversity in the kinds of gods experienced by suggesting they are just appearances of the same god. This suggestion has always struck me as bizarre. In my eyes, it's like suggesting that the appearance of a forest of trees is really just an appearance of a single tree. Why would anyone think that? Well, some have used simplicity as a reason: it is simpler to posit one god than many, and why posit more than what is needed to account for the phenomenon? But even if simplicity were an indication of truth, and simplicity was understood in the way that the monotheist needs it to be understood, we are not in a position such that we need simplicity considerations to help us see which of two competing explanations is better: we already owe these theistic perceptual experiences an initial trust.[20] Thus, we are not competing explanations of theistic perceptual experiences in order to decide which is best. In our default position, we have already endorsed their reliability.

Now, Philipse remarked that endorsing the arguments from religious experience would commit one to a swamp of gullibility. The basic idea here is that applying the principle of credulity to things like theistic perceptual experiences opens the doors to claims such as having perceived entities that most people regard as fairytale childishness. If all he is worried about is being able to maintain a healthy disbelief in these claims, applying the principle to theistic perceptual experiences would not compromise this. He specifically mentions being committed to things like goblins. Personally, I've never even heard of someone claiming to have perceived a goblin. But surely one could have good enough reason to doubt their existence to prevent such testimonies from garnishing significant support — unlike with deities. It's perfectly reasonable to have such independent skepticism of goblins (for example) so as to protect one from a swamp of gullibility.

With that we've finally reached the end of our defense of premise (2). We saw that people really do claim to have perceptual experiences of deities and that we owe such claims an initial trust. In discerning whether it is reasonable to maintain that initial trust, we examined Perceptual Objections and Prevention Objections but found all of them wanting. Since I did not, and indeed could not, examine every single possible objection to the reliability of theistic perceptual experiences, I cannot prove that premise (2) is true. However, I can, and indeed take myself to have shown that it is reasonable to believe (2): given the failure of our most formidable objections to the claim that deities have been perceived, it is unlikely that there are any good objections to the claim.

Conclusion and Summary

We began this chapter by showing that in light of the creation of our universe by a god, chances are that polytheism is true. We moved on to confirming this suspicion by presenting and defending a logically valid argument with only two premises. Its first premise merely told us what is the case if gods have been perceived, namely that polytheism is true. Its second premise, that gods have been perceived, was initially supported by the credulity we owe such claims in the absence of defeaters, but was additionally confirmed after finding that our most formidable objections to premise (2) were unable to suppress our initial credulity in it. Interestingly, we saw that monotheism is at odds with the reliability of theistic perceptual experiences.

It appears to me that we have managed to mount a reasonable case for polytheism. We have good reason to believe in the deities that have been perceived all over the world, from the Goddess experienced by Wiccans and Cernunnos by Druids, to the Hindu deities that have been experienced, and even YHWH. The gods and goddesses come in all shapes and sizes. Helix (one of 150 people interviewed by W.D. Wilkerson for her recent ethnographic research into polytheism) recounts that upon feeling 'contacted' by the goddess who had been called Isis (among other things), she and her peers responded, resulting in the following experience:

> I got the strongest single sense of presence that I'd ever had, totally terrifying and exhilarating. We got very, very strong images, and some words, and it felt like the top of my head was coming off... a lot of different physical sensations, and when we put out offerings, I visually saw something moving over the offerings as if to accept them, saw with my eyes as

opposed to just my mind's eye. So that was profound. I think I was already a polytheist at that point, but I hadn't had many of these kinds of experiences — they had had a lesser impact. This one was notable for how powerful it was and for the relationship it formed afterward. The sense of presence lingered as we continued to work with that Deity, and I continue to work with Her now. It was definitely a turning point for me.[21]

I hope that those who remain skeptical, and either doubt the truth of polytheism or actually believe its falsity, will nevertheless acknowledge that polytheism can reasonably be held by their epistemic peers. This is just to invoke the difference between the truth of a proposition and the reasons people have for believing that proposition. People may have reasons which mistakenly indicate that a belief is true. In such a case, endorsing that belief is ultimately mistaken, but nevertheless reasonable and understandable from their perspective. Finally, may polytheists feel emboldened to reclaim their intellectual residence in philosophy. Let's turn now to inquiring about the moral natures of these gods.

Chapter 4

Are The Gods Good?

Aletheia

We have managed to construct a viable natural theology in the preceding chapters. However, its content is rather bare. We will now attempt to breathe life into its skeletal structure by coming to a better understanding of the gods. In this chapter we shall endeavor to learn something interesting about the moral characters of the gods. are they good or evil? I will not invite unnecessary controversy by trying to define good and evil, and thankfully, there is no need to do so: since we can only define concepts that are already in our minds, I shall simply make appeal to those pre-theorized concepts. While goodness and evil are certainly not exhausted by virtue and vice, they surely involve them. A good way to understand our initial question then is whether or not the gods are kind, patient, or deceitful; conscientious, resentful or selfish, and so forth.

Bearing this in mind, it will be helpful to begin our inquiry by drawing a distinction not unlike that between matter and form. We apprehend this distinction in our experience as the difference between a thing's essence and its existence, between *what* it is (or would be) and *whether* it is. That something exists is one thing, but what it is that exists is quite another. Essence is what makes a thing the sort of thing that it is, whereas existence is what makes a thing to be. This is how we are able to coherently talk about things that don't exist, such as fictional characters. Without any difficulty, we are able to conceive of non-existent things like the Chimaera, Sphinx, Dragon, and even Superman. The distinct conception of each thing that we have in mind is just the form or essence which, if instantiated, would make it to be that thing.

The essences of almost everything in our experience are such as to be this or that sort of thing, but not just *to be*: their essences need to be made to exist. For example, it is not a part of our essence that we exist. This is why humans come into and go out of existence, for their essence is one thing, their existence another; and their essence has not always been (nor will it always be) made to exist. To illustrate the distinction further, you might say that existence is something that *happened* to the essence of humanity, thereby requiring the two to be different.

As can be seen from the foregoing, without essence, existence is not anything, for to be anything at all is to be individuated, and that is just to have essence. Incidentally, this is why medieval philosophers would quip that existence does not exist, for all by itself, it doesn't! Moreover, without existence essence does not...exist. So, we may gather that existence and essence are distinct, co-dependent components of things, or in other words, that things tend to be constituted by their essence and existence.

But something must explain why two different things, *viz.* an essence and its existence, are united together, and we can only say this union is due to one of three things:

(i): The essence or its existence in isolation from the other
(ii): The essence and its existence in conjunction with one another
(iii): Something other than the essence and its existence

However, (i) is impossible because as noted, apart from existence, an essence doesn't exist nor is existence apart from essence a thing, let alone one that could explain this union. Moreover, (ii) is impossible since cause logically precedes effect and the conjunction of an essence with its existence cannot logically precede itself. Therefore, every union of essence and existence is due to an external cause. In fact, no substance so composed can last a single instant unless it is conserved in existence by an external cause, otherwise its essence and existence would need to be unified in terms of either (i) or (ii). The medievals called this the Doctrine of Divine Conservation. It is opposed by the idea of existential inertia, which has it that a being in existence will tend to stay in existence until caused not to.

Given the foregoing, what could be sustaining all of these incomprehensibly many substances at any given moment? Well, whatever else we may say about it, because it is external to this entire series of substances, it cannot be a composition of essence and existence. That is, its essence is not *united* with its existence; its essence *is* its existence. This entity is therefore permanent in the strongest sense of the term: it cannot possibly have come into existence, nor could it possibly, under any circumstances whatsoever, stop existing, for its essence just is to exist.

We might still wonder, however, about what exactly this deity is. But this natural curiosity should not be born of the belief that something needs to be made out of stuff in order to exist, for as we saw, matter without form is simply nothing. We may draw from this the lesson that what makes something real, in a constitutional sense (call it 'being'), needn't be quantifiable stuff. Things have being in radically different ways: substances like you and I have it in a more independent way than properties like colors, which only exist through other things. Moreover, we have being in a material way, while many gods do not. But while each of us only 'has' being, this deity does not. We merely 'have' being because it is given to us, whereas nothing gives this deity being, as if its essence needed to be conjoined with being in order to exist. Rather, its essence is its existence, and therefore it just is being. This needn't mean that it is being in all its myriad forms, for being preceded those forms. It simply means that it is more real than any of us could possibly fathom: our lives are just half-remembered dreams by comparison.

Moreover, there could not be, even in principle, more than one such entity, for there would be no individuation between them: they would be the very same thing. Interestingly, Thomas

Aquinas argued otherwise. On the basis of his belief that this deity (whom he called 'God') had specially revealed through Christianity that it is a trinity of persons, Aquinas attempted to argue that such a trinitarian nature is not incompatible with this god's radical unity. Note the negative nature of his argument: it is not that we have any philosophical reason to think 'God' is a trinity of persons, just that there's no reason to think God isn't a trinity of persons. This is cohesive with a remark he makes about disputing the doctrines of revealed theology with non-believers:

> If our opponent believes nothing of divine revelation, there is no longer any means of proving the articles of faith by reasoning, but only of answering his objections — if he has any — against faith. Since faith rests upon infallible truth, and since the contrary of a truth can never be demonstrated, it is clear that the arguments brought against faith cannot be demonstrations, but are difficulties that can be answered.[1]

As mentioned in chapter one, Aquinas said relations exist within this god, and the persons of the Trinity just are those relations. Bill Craig and J.P. Moreland summarize this extremely difficult idea well: 'Because the one knowing generates the one known and they share the same essence, they are related as Father to Son. Moreover, God loves himself, so that God as beloved is relationally distinct from God as loving'.[2] But they proceed to raise insuperable difficulties for this idea, including everything from commonsensical objections like 'it's not intelligible to say that persons are relations: relations don't know truths or love people', and 'there's no better reason to think the individual denoted by 'I', 'me' and 'myself' are different persons in God's case than in ours' to the charge of internal-inconsistency: 'Thomas's doctrine of the Trinity is doubtless inconsistent with his doctrine of divine simplicity. Intuitively, it seems obvious that a being that is absolutely without composition and transcends all distinctions cannot have real relations subsisting within it, much less be three distinct persons'.[3] I will therefore assume that this deity is not a trinity of persons. I shall call this deity Aletheia, since she simply *is* reality at its very roots.

Aletheia's Creations

While this may teach us something interesting about the god who ultimately created the universe, how is it relevant to an inquiry about the moral characters of the gods? Well, because if there is goodness and evil (as our experience surely attests), they will have essences, otherwise goodness and evil would be indistinguishable from each other and anything else. Moreover, they will either be compositions of their essences and existence, or they will not. If they are so composed, then like every other such thing, Aletheia creates them and conserves them in existence. But if their essences and existence do not form a composition because they are not actually different, then goodness and evil must be identical with Aletheia, for there can only be one such entity.

Now it does not seem that Aletheia could unify the essences of either goodness or evil with existence, for the action of causing good is itself good, and that of causing evil itself bad. (This is not to speak of the value or disvalue of an action's consequences, but of the action itself.) Thus, these values would need to exist, being exemplified by the causal act itself, prior to being created by this act — a clear impossibility. However, in so far as their essences are different from their existence, Aletheia will have needed to create them; for no such composite can last a single instant unless it is conserved in existence by Aletheia. It follows that because Aletheia could not have created them, their essences are not distinct from their existence, or in other words, that it is of their essences to exist. But this can hardly count as progress, for how can goodness and evil be identical with Aletheia? This is just to say that Aletheia is good and not good, evil and not evil. And as the law of non-contradiction states, no proposition can be both true and false. So it is impossible for her to be essentially both good and evil. Otherwise, the proposition that Aletheia is good will be both true and false. It would seem that there are only two ways out of the corner that we have been backed into. Either there really is no goodness or evil, or only one of them exists. For, in so far as either exists, we are forced back into considering how its essence and existence relate to Aletheia.

Now, I take the former option to be simply unacceptable: is there *really* nothing good about love, mercy and hope? Nothing evil about abusing children or animals? Any argument to the contrary will fail to be as plausible as the reality is that abuse is evil. We are then forced, it seems to me, to conclude that either goodness or evil are not actually any substantive thing. One or the other is like a hole in the ground or a doughnut: it's not so much a thing in its own right, but rather the absence of a thing. Traditionally theists have argued that evil does not properly exist, but is rather a privation of something that does. Evil is the corruption or perversion of goodness, and surely this seems intuitive. Evil is naturally thought of as perverse and corrupt, both of which presuppose there is something which has been corrupted or perverted. It is difficult to even conceive of an evil that is not parasitic upon some good. E.g. lying is the perversion of honesty, hatred of love, bigotry of tolerance and so forth. Moreover, if goodness were the value that did not exist, then we would have to understand things like happiness, joy, truth and beauty as parasitic upon various pre-existing evils, and it is just too easy to conceive of such things existing in a world without any evils whatsoever. Since logically prior to creating anything at all, one of these values must have existed in isolation from the other; we have best reason to think it was goodness.

However, if goodness is the value that exists, then it must be identical with Aletheia. That is, goodness and Aletheia must really just be one and the same thing. As we have sound reason to believe that there is goodness, we may therefore conclude this remarkable deduction by identifying Aletheia with goodness.

It may be difficult to understand what it means to say that the essence of goodness and of Aletheia are the same, so let us spend a few minutes orienting ourselves to this thought. At its roots all that is being said is that the terms 'goodness' and 'Aletheia' refer to the very same thing, and that this thing is being, or in other words, that in virtue of which anything at all is real. However, while 'goodness' refers to 'being', it does so in its capacity as that recognizable but beautifully enigmatic form hidden in the virtues. 'Aletheia', on the other hand, refers to 'being' in its capacity as the fountainhead of all reality. Put another way, goodness does not refer to being *qua* being, but rather to something like being *qua* desirable, or *qua* admirable. This is much in the same way that 'Clark Kent' refers to the same individual that 'Superman' does, but the former *qua* civilian and the latter *qua* hero. Likewise, while a mother and her son are both referring to the very same man when the former says 'my husband' and the latter 'my dad', they are referring to him in different capacities.

We argued earlier that goodness involves the virtues. However, it is quite apparent that many different things are virtuous. For example, courage, honesty, and justice are each virtuous, and therefore good. How then can such different things really be one and the same? This question exploits an ambiguity in grammar: the difference between predicating and identifying. We have argued that goodness is to be identified with Aletheia, not that it is to be predicated of her. She is not just an exemplar of goodness; she is its very locus. Predicating goodness would involve goodness being other than her. By contrast, goodness is predicated of things like courage, honesty and justice, not identified with them: they exemplify goodness, but do not constitute it. Thus, it has not been said that all these diverse things are one and the same, but rather that they have some attribute in common, namely goodness.

It is remarkable to think that Aletheia permeates all of reality. Her life courses through the world's veins. And she has honored us by plunging her arm into non-existence, and drawing us, of all people, into the warmth of being. As the root of reality, she is as far removed from us as anything could possibly be. And yet, by shielding us from the ever-threatening tides of non-existence, there's no one closer to us than she.

The Euthyphro Dilemma

Having identified a god with the good, we are led squarely into what has plagued philosophy for thousands of years: Euthyphro's dilemma. This phrase refers to a sort of objection paradigmatically represented by Socrates' question to the pagan priest Euthyphro: 'do the gods will what is good because it is good, or is it good because they will it?'. This dilemma has been rephrased in a variety of ways over the years, but represents a kind of objection that often gets posed to theists wishing to identify a god with the good.

The problem is concerned with how the given deity is supposed to relate to the goodness of things, and both options seem to land the theist in a very uncomfortable, untenable position. On the one hand, if their deity wills what is good because it is good, then there is a standard of goodness independent of that deity, and she cannot be said to be identical with goodness, nor embody its fullness and so forth. On the other hand, if things are good because their deity wills them to be, then goodness is a consequence of their god's will. But since cause logically precedes effect, this would require that the deity logically precedes goodness, and therefore fails to be identical with it. Moreover, this implies that whatever the deity wills, no matter what, it would thereby be good. So, if the deity willed dishonesty, infidelity, or any other given perversion of a good, it would be good! But that's absurd.

Some theists have responded by embracing one or the other of these routes. For example, William of Ockham infamously endorsed the second and vigorously defended an extreme form of the Divine Command Theory — according to which God's commands make things morally right or wrong, no matter what they are. Still, others such as Richard Swinburne have taken the first route and argued that morality is logically necessary, thus existing quite independently of any and all gods.

More usually, however, theists reject the whole thing altogether and propose a third option. Before taking a look at possible third options, allow me to evaluate the dilemma in light of the particular view being developed here. Let's word this dilemma as follows:

Either Aletheia wills things because they are good, or things are good because she wills them to be.

We may reject the first disjunct right off the bat: Aletheia does not will things because they are good. Why? Because, if goodness were independent of Aletheia, then its essence would be different than its existence and Aletheia would have to create it. But this is impossible, for the act of creating goodness would itself be good. Thus, the essence of goodness must be one with its existence, and therefore (since there can only be one such thing) with Aletheia. Moreover, the second disjunct is false as well. Goodness is not an effect of Aletheia, for then its essence would be distinct from its existence. Since a disjunctive statement is true if and only if at least one of its disjuncts are true, it is reasonable for us to conclude that the dilemma is a false one. Perhaps there is no need to go further and construct a third alternative: it is not as if the dilemma will somehow revive itself if we fail to do so.

However, it is good to know that there are alternatives that have been developed. So, how might Aletheia relate to the goodness of things? Well, just as we might say the plethora of triangles we encounter in our experience, such as those drawn on sidewalks or those within architecture, count as triangles because they instantiate the essence of triangularity (*albeit* imperfectly), so too might the good things of our experience imperfectly instantiate the essence of goodness. But we need not try and figure out how she relates to the goodness of things, it's enough to know that she does.

Gods Come From Goodness

We have deduced that Aletheia is not only the creator of gods, but is supremely good. We might therefore expect that whatever she does, including creating a deity, is good. This is not to say that every creature made by Aletheia is perfectly good. Human beings are anything but perfect! And it is from this reality that we may draw an important lesson: Aletheia's nature no more rules out imperfect deities than it does imperfect humans. But this still leaves us with a *prima facie* reason to expect a given deity to be good. True, a deity could develop evil dispositions over time: don't we as well? But we cannot accept that this has actually happened in advance of any reason to think so. Our default position is thus to believe that a given deity has retained its initial goodness.

The Problem of Evil

Often atheists will look to our universe and repel at the thought of a perfectly good deity having created it. Lifeless, hostile, and cold...wouldn't we expect better from such a deity? And perhaps they are right! Aletheia may not have directly created the universe. She may instead have allowed a created deity to bring about the universe. In such a case, she would have sustained everything in existence while the created deity exerted a much narrower scope of causation, say by initiating the Big Bang and the ensuing universe, that took billions of years of empty space and black holes until biological life emerged. Just as she permits us to struggle with our imperfections, she permits deities to struggle with theirs.

The theoretical approach taken by the atheist just described above represents the infamous Problem of Evil. The arguments from evil are widely considered to be the strongest arguments for atheism. How on Earth, the argument might go, could a god just stand by and let an innocent child starve to death? Moreover, it would have taken but the lifting of a finger for a god to raze the Nazi regime to the ground. They wouldn't need to be perfect, just decent.

However, the arguments we have enlisted on behalf of theism and polytheism made no reference to the moral characters of any deities. Thus, their soundness was established quite indepen dently of the problems of evil. At most, such problems would inform us that no gods are good, but they certainly won't show that there are no gods. How could they do that? Aletheia is supremely good.

Normally, problems of evil would be divided into two broad camps according to how strongly they take the tension between the existence of evil (or suffering) and the existence of some deity to be. Logical problems of evil allege that the tension is so strong that it's actually a contradiction. In other words, they say the co-existence of evil and some kind of good god(s) are impossible. The evidential problems of evil, on the other hand, merely claim that evil (or suffering) counts as evidence against the existence of a morally appropriate god.

With a few notable exceptions, most philosophers today acknowledge that there is no contradiction between a good deity existing and the existence of evil or suffering. The focus has thus noticeably shifted to evidential problems of evil. This latter sort come in a variety of forms: some deductive, others inductive; some focusing on a particular instance of evil, others on the totality of it. What they allege in common is that we should expect the existence of some evil or suffering (from now on, just 'evil') more, given that atheism is true than that there is a good deity that could prevent it. But as indicated above, the preceding arguments show that evil and suffering should not at all be expected under atheism, for there could not even be a universe (let alone one with evil in it) unless a god kept its matter and form united. In fact, it is because no essence could be united to existence without Aletheia that there cannot be any evidence for atheism, even in principle. For the only thing that atheism predicts is that there is nothing at all, and if there were nothing, then, *a fortiori*, there would be no evidence.

Now, since we are interested in the moral characters of the gods, we shall try not to dismiss the problems of evil, but rather to redirect them to help us. However, it is admittedly difficult to know how to do this, since we cannot reinterpret them so as to argue that some evil is more likely given that the gods are not good than given that they are. Again, Aletheia is supremely good. Perhaps the best course of action is to take them to be concerned with all created deities. However, we would need to be sure that a created deity was responsible for the evil. Otherwise, the evil may not be directly due to any agent at all, or not to a divine agent at least. To simplify matters, let's pretend that Aletheia isn't good, or at least that we have no good reason to think so. On this basis, let us proceed to see whether the problems of evil can inform us about the moral characters of the gods.

There are at least two reasons why we should be very cautious about inferring which evils a deity would prevent because of its good nature. The first is that while a good moral character may incline a deity to prevent some evil, a greater good might incline it to permit that evil. Allowing an evil to take place so that a greater good may result is a morally sufficient reason to allow that evil. Thus, in order to reasonably say a good god would have prevented such-and-such an evil, we need to know that the deity wouldn't have allowed it for the sake of a greater good. But how do we know that in preventing an evil, the deity wouldn't be forfeiting a greater good? Sometimes, theists argue that we're not really in a good enough position to know such things (no matter the armchair), and therefore that it's not reasonable to argue that the deity would prevent the evil: for all we know, there is a greater good which would incline it to do so. This position is (broadly) known as skeptical-theism.[5] Atheists have responded by highlighting alleged untoward implications of such skepticism; such as that we couldn't know when any action was right or wrong, for it's always possible that there is a greater good out there. But the reasons for being skeptical about our knowledge concerning the greater goods available to gods do not apply to our knowledge concerning the greater goods available to humans. Other theists have more ambitiously tried to identify which greater goods would be lost if the evil in question were prevented, such as free will. These are more or less the Orthodox avenues for a theist to take when grappling with the evidential problems of evil.

However, I shall take another route, and it begins with what I'm sure many will find to be an uncomfortable observation: honest and hardworking people regularly choose to buy luxuries instead of alleviating the suffering of the less fortunate. And yet, choosing luxury over alleviating suffering (and saving lives, in many cases) does not in and of itself make one a bad person. Many of us remain patient, honest, courageous and prudent despite how we spend our surplus. Of course, we might fairly be accused of *behaving* unjustly, selfishly or even negligently in doing so, but we are not thereby guilty of *being* unjust, selfish or negligent persons. Things are not so black or white. This little detail sheds enormous light on the problems of evil: it would seem the gods are no more wicked or callous for not intervening than we are. By itself, a good moral character is not sufficient to make one intervene and prevent evil. We are therefore not justified in saying that a given deity would prevent some evil because of its good character — we need more information.

So, what is the missing ingredient? What must be added to a

good moral character to incline someone to prevent an evil? As interesting and serious as these questions are, it must be kept in mind that our failure or even inability to answer them would not mean that there is no missing ingredient. If anything, it would just mean we need to look deeper. I say this not to hedge my bets but to place the onus where it belongs: on the skeptic's shoulders. Having said that, I think there are some plausible answers out there. For example, perhaps good agents freely choose to prevent evil when they have a sense of responsibility for whether or not the evil obtains.[6] This may be what triggers the good dispositions in people and compels them into action. I know from my own experience that when I feel it's up to me whether or not an evil obtains, I am compelled to intervene; but when I do not feel responsible, the urgency evaporates.

This is of course a tentative suggestion. Perhaps it does not suffice to explain why a good agent freely intervenes. She may feel responsible as I have described, but nevertheless intervene for a different reason. Whatever the case, the fact of the matter seems to be that having a good moral character does not really tell us what actions one is likely to perform or to avoid. Thus, it does not seem the problems of evil are very useful tools for our inquiry.

Alternative Methods?

We have seen that there is some reason to presume the gods to be good until it is shown otherwise, and that no gods could be purely evil. Unfortunately, theorizing does not seem to get us much further than speculation on this issue. At some point, we will need to get our hands dirty in the details of experience. After all, we can speculate about how some abstractly conceived human being behaves until we go blue in the face, but our primary source for learning about people's moral characters will remain experience. And experiences of the gods reveal a startling array of moral characters: some Wiccans describe the presence of the Goddess as overwhelmingly loving, some Druids sense a wild and fiercely protective nature in Cernunnos, and Christians a terrifying and enraged nature in Lucifer. Gods and goddesses appear as everything from erotically sexual to deeply concerned. It's hard to nail any of them down as 'good' or 'bad', but perhaps that shouldn't surprise us.

Chapter 5

Unanswered Questions

The Hinge

We have covered a lot of ground and ploughed through a lot of abstract thought, so let's take a breather and try to draw the major themes together, as well as discuss some potentially fruitful areas of study worth pursuing in the future. In a lot of ways, the distinctively Aristotelian case for polytheism developed here relied on Aletheia as a hinge. It was through the inability of material substances to exist without being sustained by her that our case for theism rested. And our case for polytheism of course hinges on our case for theism. Moreover, it was through the dependence of things composed of essence and existence upon Aletheia that we discovered she is good in the purest of senses. And this conclusion allowed us to effectively refute the arguments from evil as well as the Euthyphro Dilemma. Further, as we shall soon see, reflecting on Aletheia's relationship to the other gods could prove inestimably informative with respect to how the gods relate to one another.

Costs and Benefits

Given the substantial role she plays in the worldview I've described, it is only fair to discuss the difficulties this might cause for some. The place of a 'source' like Aletheia in polytheist belief has mixed reviews. Certainly, many polytheists have and do believe in such a deity. For example, in Zoroastrianism, Ahura Mazda plays a very similar role, as does Rod according to some forms of Rodnovery. And of course, we mustn't forget that Aristotle was a pagan. But many others do not. For example, such a deity seems to have a difficult time finding a place in the cosmology of Norse polytheism. However, accepting the existence of Aletheia should only amplify one's worldview: it is to admit that the utmost level of reality is Deity, and that she burns with goodness. It seems to me then that the reasons we've adduced for believing in her existence should not only be accepted for their strength, but enthusiastically so because of their implication.

While we are on this topic, I should acknowledge how uncomfortable affirming the existence of gods traditionally associated with monotheism may make some polytheists. However, people have had perceptual experiences of them, and thus, we have good reason to believe they exist. Of course, this needn't commit one to believing what various texts say about these gods. That would be like demanding we believe whatever the Eddas say about Odin just because he has appeared to some. Likewise, I realize that many Christians will be uncomfortable saying Aletheia is not Trinitarian. They will of course be the only ones who can weigh whether their reasons for interpreting the Bible so as to teach that God is a Trinity are as strong as the reasons here given for denying that she is. However, I do want to interject that natural theology precedes revealed theology in the sense that something can only be trusted to be a divine revelation in so far as one has reason to believe in the divinity who is the purported author. Thus, if reason tells us God cannot be a Trinity, we have strong reason to believe that God has not revealed that he is.

The Divine Society

Let us turn now to reflecting on some areas which concern polytheism, and may prove quite fruitful in future studies. This final section of the book will be the most speculative, but I hope it gives the reader a glimmer of just how much more interesting work is left to be done. I have approached many of the questions in this book from a distinctively Aristotelian perspective. But there are many other schools of thought, each bringing with them answers that range from the subtly different to the completely opposed. I encourage the reader to bring his or her own philo-sophical lineage to the table, whether that be Platonist, Lockean, Kantian or whatever it may be, and help us to unravel some of these puzzles.

It is a curious thing that the gods co-exist. How do they relate to one another? Do they form a society? If so, how is it stratified? Is there a Divine Government that rules this society? If so, how does it operate? The questions are as endless as they are intriguing. The issue is only complicated by the myriad of relationships we experience and learn of amongst ourselves, for they simply add to the possibilities. Often, these relationships are used to model those of the gods, such as in mythology. There we encounter a rich diversity of tales covering the politics of life as a god. Practically every pre-industrial society had a pantheon with whom they related to: Egyptian, Greek, Roman, Aztec, Sumerian, and Chinese, you name it. Perhaps we can extrapolate literal truths from these tales, especially in so far as they roman-ticize information retrieved through perceptual experiences of the gods. However, our focus will remain on what philosophy can tell us.

Property Rights

Let's reflect on Aletheia's relationship with her creations in the hope that this will shed light on how the gods relate to one another. Consider first whether or not she has property rights over creation. Surely, in some sense, the world is *hers*. After all, she brings it into being, sustains it there, and allows it, at any point she deems fit, to cease. Now, if we think we humans sometimes own the result of rearranging pre-existent matter, how much more should we think she owns her product, she who does infinitely more than just moving blocks around into new shapes?

If I were to have an apartment complex built, it would be thought that I had certain rights over that property: I could lease it to others, or have them evicted. Folks would not just come off the streets to start building something else there in its place, and if they did, I could easily have them escorted off the property by police officers. Moreover, it would be considered wrongful of others to capriciously destroy the building, or make unsanctioned use of it. Now, I'm not going to try and untangle our intuitions about why one would suddenly acquire rights over chunks of matter after having them arranged in a certain pattern. But I want to suggest that what is good for the goose is good for the gander. If we are entitled to stake our claim on a plot of land because we got there 'first', or because someone who is related to us within an arbitrarily defined proximity got there 'first', how much more should it be the case that Aletheia has claim over reality, she who is First?

This suggestion obviously has its limits. People are not the sorts of things we can own: slavery is morally reprehensible. Nor, does it seem, can we come to own certain things that people produce without their permission. For example, I am not permitted to take your vehicle unless I have your permission. To do otherwise is theft. You might loan it to me or even sell it to me, but barring extremely extenuating circumstances, I will need your permission. From these points we might come to the conclusion that Aletheia does not own people or gods, nor certain things they produce (for we have surely not given Aletheia permission to take everything of ours, especially if we are atheists?). On the flipside, we might start to wonder whether we have wronged Aletheia by making unsanctioned use of her products, or by abusing them. Undoubtedly, our careless destruction of natural resources is an egregious affront, not just to each other and our future generations, but ultimately to Aletheia, and to those deities who are more directly connected to these resources.

Unless she has made it known otherwise, the morally safe position to take is to assume that we do not own our natural resources. That is, we are but privileged stewards at best, and we owe her property respect. We would not carelessly dump toxins or other wastes on to our boss' front lawn, nor on the workspace that our boss has provided for us. Why then do we do so to Aletheia? Who among us, upon being entrusted with the care of their neighbor's animal for the weekend, would proceed to hunt it for sport? And yet, there is hardly an animal on this planet that humanity has not hunted for sport. Now, I do not intend for this section to be a tirade against the corrupt attitudes humankind has formed toward the Earth, its eco-systems and so forth. Instead, I want to draw lessons from our behavior about how the gods behave. We may expect that they are aware of Aletheia's property rights, and thereby have reason to behave in certain ways. For example, a god may be unlikely to disrupt the law-like regularities of nature, for to do so would be to make unsanctioned use of Aletheia's property. And the plot only thickens when it comes to morally significant reasons for interfering with nature. On the one hand, a deity may be morally permitted to overrule Aletheia's property rights if, for example, lives are at stake. But, on the other hand, perhaps humankind has placed themselves in such a position that no injustice would be done by letting nature run her course. These are tough questions that deserve much more thought.

Divine Providence

What is the purpose of creation? Perhaps we can answer this by inquiring about the motives of creation. Given Aletheia's nature as pure and unadulterated goodness, there can be no good that is greater than or independent of her. Thus, there would be no good she would want or need to acquire for her own sake, let alone through creation. In fact, it seems the only good she must will of necessity is her own, for her own good *is* goodness. Thus, anything she wills beside herself must be freely willed. But why would she freely choose to create when this would not acquire a good she wanted or needed for her own sake? It would seem the only answer available is that creation was not for her sake at all, but for creation's. That is, her act was completely selfless and oriented toward the good of creation. We might therefore gather that there is a purpose to creation, and it lies in its own flourishing or some such.

Divine Government

We mentioned above the possibility of a Divine Government. We might fear that this inquiry could be used for political means. After all, if the gods have chosen such-and-such a form of government, who are we to choose differently? However, such an inquiry is still important, and should no more be ignored because of potential misuses than any other. This question doesn't need to be treated so parochially as to be concerned with whether the gods have annual elections or paid holidays. More realistically, the question relates to pecking orders: are any gods in charge of others? One might be in charge of others in a variety of different ways depending on the kind of authority possessed.

Where this authority is to be understood in political terms, we may look to political philosophy for help. For example, assuming that there is a human government with political authority, where does it derive its authority from? Whatever answer we come up with, perhaps it applies by analogy to the gods. Some have suggested that governments derive their authority to rule from the consent of their citizens. This family of so-called 'social contract' theories have it that the citizens of a state and their government enter into a contractual agreement: the state maintains order and provides security while the people promise obedience to the laws. Of course, this needs to be qualified in some way because no such contract explicitly exists. That is, no government official goes around trying to obtain signatures so that people will obey the laws: the cops are going to pull you over for speeding regardless of whether or not you signed. Thus, the terms of this agreement must be implicit, perhaps assumed by the behavior of the citizens. For example, it has been suggested that citizens implicitly agree to submit to the government by remaining in a given territory. Granted, this would be irrelevant unless the government owns that territory. But perhaps the gods implicitly agree to submit to Aletheia by remaining in a given region of the universe. Again, others have suggested that citizens implicitly agree to a government's power by making use of its goods and services. Where these goods and services include ubiquitous things like public roads, this again supposes that a government has legitimate property rights over that territory, and didn't simply take the land through conquest or purchase it with illegitimately acquired funds. This problem does not seem to pertain to the gods, however. And of course, there are many different ideas about how a government derives the political authority it is thought to have. While I confess to being mystified about the idea that a government has such authority, I want to suggest that analogies could be drawn. That is, if human societies lack political authority because of x, y or z, then perhaps divine societies do as well. And likewise, *vice versa*.

However, our initial question may be understood in terms other than politics, such as morality. We may rephrase the question accordingly: are any gods morally in charge of others? A god might have moral authority in the sense that her decrees carry the weight of moral obligations, or in the sense that she knows of what she speaks. The latter sense is quite familiar to us: people acquire advanced degrees on subjects, and become an authority on the matter, qualified to speak as an expert. But I take the former to be more interesting than the latter when it comes to the gods, for the latter seems trivially true: of course the gods are authorities on moral matters, they probably are on matters in general. The former seems to be more substantive in that learning of it would be deeply informative. This more ontological sense of moral authority has been the meat of Divine Command Theories, according to which 'God' (or some relevant deity) creates moral obligations through commanding and forbidding certain actions. Older versions stipulated that a deity created moral values as well, but this risked making morality arbitrary, for a god who creates both moral duties and values has no moral duties or values prior to doing so, and thus could create whatever values or duties it pleased. But this seems absurd; no matter how hard a deity may try, it simply cannot make rape good, or wellbeing evil. Contemporary versions stipulate that the deity in question grounds moral value in a very constitutional way: she either perfectly exemplifies it, or just is it. This constrains which actions she can command or forbid, although this would not be because of any moral duties on her part, but because of how her values dispose her to act. But why would a god's commands generate moral obligations?

David Baggett and Jerry Walls opine:

[L]et us consider the reasons we normally ascribe authority to someone. Sometimes it is a simple matter of power. A person who has the legal power to enforce his will, for instance, has a certain kind of authority. Another source of authority is knowledge and information. We recognize as authorities those persons who have sufficient mastery of a field of discipline that they can command respect for what they know and understand. A third source of morality is moral integrity and character, the sort of authority that appeals to our conscience and demands respect in a deeper sense than the authority that comes from mere power, or even knowledge. Indeed a person who has mere power or legal authority but who lacks moral integrity, lacks the authority to command our respect — even if he has the power to enforce his will on us. Now then, God has supreme power, knowledge, and goodness, and all of these underwrite his moral authority.[1]

If this line of reasoning held, then the gods would be ruled in a moral sense by Aletheia, as would we and any other recipient of the divine commands. However, I have outlined grounds for being skeptical that the first two senses of authority are relevant to, and the third needs considerable unpacking.

Delegation

Then there is what we could call the Distribution Hypothesis. This is the thesis that the highest deity has divided creation up and distributed it among the gods. Here the gods are allotted responsibility over some portion of creation, and this responsibility may be conceived in either moral or political terms. Interestingly, this hypothesis has been advanced for thousands of years all over the globe. For example, Deuteronomy 32 makes an interesting claim:

> This family of the divine arrangement of the world appears also in the versions of Deuteronomy 32:8-9 preserved in Greek (Septuagint) and the Dead Sea Scrolls:
>
> > When the Most High (Elyon) allotted peoples for inheritance,
> > When He divided up humanity,
> > He fixed the boundaries for peoples,
> > According to the number of the divine sons:
> > For Yahweh's portion is his people,
> > Jacob His own inheritance.

The traditional Hebrew text (Masoretic text, or MT) perhaps reflects a discomfort with this polytheistic theology of Israel, for it shows not 'divine sons' (bene elohim), as in the Greek and the Dead Sea Scrolls, but 'sons of Israel' (bene yisrael). E. Tov labels the MT text here an 'anti-polytheistic alteration'. The texts of the Septuagint and the Dead Sea Scrolls show Israelite polytheism which focuses on the central importance of Yahweh for Israel within the larger scheme of the world;

yet this larger scheme provides a place for other gods of the other nations of the world... This worldview was cast as the divine patrimonial household in Deuteronomy 32: each god held his own inheritance, and the whole was headed by the patriarchal god. Other gods in their nations represented no threat to Israel and its patron god as long as they were not imported into Israel. As long as other gods did not affect worship of Yahweh in Israel, they could be tolerated as the gods of other peoples and nations.[2]

The OT specialist and John O' Brian Professor Emeritus of Biblical Studies at Notre Dame, Joseph Blenkinsopp agrees: 'The idea is that Elyon, high god of the Canaanite pantheon, assigned each of the 70 nations of the world (Gen 10) to one of the 70 deities of the pantheon and that Israel had the good fortune to be assigned Yahweh'.[3]

Finally, the early polytheist critic of Christianity, Celsus, says something very similar to Deuteronomy 32:8-9. In Origen's *Contra Celsus* Book 5, Chapter 25 Celsus says that 'in all probability, the various quarters of the Earth were from the beginning allotted to different superintending spirits, and were thus distributed among certain governing powers, and in this manner the administration of the world is carried on'.

This may help explain why there were believed to be regional pantheons: because there were. We might also add that it would be fitting for Aletheia to assign a portion of reality to a god who has a relevantly similar nature. For example, if a god has a particularly strong influence over water (like our influence over neural-matter), Aletheia might task her with responsibilities concerning water. This would correlate well with what has been said about Aletheia's property rights. We noted in chapter two that every agent acts for an end. That is, causes are pre-disposed to produce certain effects (or ranges thereof). This simple principle explains the regularity we observe in nature: cells divide because their pre-disposition to do so becomes realized. The reality of such pre-dispositions is why acorns regularly become oak trees, why gestation follows a normal course, and even why planets continually orbit. But what if a god's pre-dispositions include producing something that is highly specific to a region of reality? It would be fitting for Aletheia to direct her to that region.

As we remarked in the beginning of this chapter, these matters are extremely speculative. Yet, they are fascinating and deserve further exploration. Whether or not we have succeeded in putting some meat on our case for polytheism, we do have a case for polytheism — and it is only one, in what I hope will become a great variety of cases.

Endnotes

Chapter 1: What is a God?

1. Waterfield (2000. p.xi)
2. Interestingly, it seems Christians have been in a similar predicament before: 'I do not suppose that anyone in the fifteenth or sixteenth centuries was a pagan, in the sense of rejecting Christianity and adopting a pre-Christian religion... What I do suggest is that some people during this period 'dreamed' of being pagans'. – Godwin (2005. p.2) as cited by Myers (2013. p108)
3. Philipse (2012. p.3)
4. This state can be reached through numerous meditative techniques, but my favorite comes from the oldest Buddhist tradition, the Theravada, and is called vipassana.
5. By 'intuition', I do not mean some sort of assertive gut feeling. Rather, I follow Michael Huemer's analysis: 'The way things seem prior to reasoning we may call an 'initial appearance'. An initial, intellectual appearance is an 'intuition'. That is, an intuition that p is a state of its seeming to one that p that is not dependent on inference from other beliefs and that results from thinking about p, as opposed to perceiving, remembering, or introspecting'. – Huemer (2005. pp.101-2)
6. Hatcher (1985. p.74)
7. Taliaferro (2010. p.292)
8. Murray (1998. p.3)
9. Willis (2006. p.24)
10. In *Summa Theologica* (P. 1, Q. 40, A. 2), Aquinas says 'The persons are the subsisting relations themselves'.
11. Moreland & Craig (2003. pp.591-92)

Chapter 2: Is There a God?

1. Lewis (1991. pp.81-2)
2. Feser (2009. p.13)
3. Oderberg (2007. p.82)
4. Aquinas, *Summa Contra Gentiles*, Book 3, Chap. 2. in Pegis (1948, p.431)
5. In case the reader feels that in claiming there are non-physical mental phenomena, I have illicitly smuggled theistic beliefs such as immaterial minds into the argument, note that the overwhelming majority of philosophers of mind (who are atheists) believe in irreducibly mental phenomena. 'The conventional view in contemporary philosophy of mind is that even though all things are materially constituted, mental properties and events are distinct from and in some sense irreducible to physical ones'. – McLaughlin & Cohen (2007. p.243)
6. *Cf.* Swinburne (2004. p.22)

Chapter 3: How Many Gods Are There?

1. For example, Thomas Aquinas argued that 'If then many gods existed, they would necessarily differ from each other. Something therefore would belong to one that did not belong to another. And if this were a privation, one of them would not be absolutely perfect; but if a perfection, one of them would be without it. So it is impossible for many gods to exist'. – Aquinas, *Summa Theologica* P. 1, Q. 11, A. 3. in Pegis (1948, p.67)

   John Damascus also argued: 'The Deity is perfect, and without blemish in goodness, and wisdom, and power, without beginning, without end, everlasting, uncircumscribed, and in short, perfect in all things. Should we say, then, that there are many Gods, we must recognize difference among the many. For if there is no difference among them, they are one rather than many. But if there is difference among them, what becomes of the perfectness? For that which comes short of perfection, whether it be in goodness, or power, or wisdom, or time, or place, could not be God'. – *Exposition of the Orthodox Faith*, Book 1, Chapter 5.

2 Greer (2005. p.55)

3. John Damascus (*Exposition of the Orthodox Faith*, Book 1, Chapter 5)

4. 'I suggest that it is a principle of rationality that (in the absence of special considerations), if it seems (epistemically) to a subject that x is present (and has some characteristic), then probably x is present (and has that characteristic); what one seems to perceive is probably so.' – Swinburne (2004. p.303)

5. 'Other things being equal, it is reasonable to assume that things are the way they appear.' – Huemer, (2005. p.99) *Cf.* Huemer's extensive defense of this in his (2001, pp.99-115.)

6. Wall, (1995. p.50)

7. James (1902, pp.67-8)

8. Alexander (2012)

9. Audi (2007. p.134) On page 146, Audi says 'For Hume, our 'assurance' in any matter depending on testimony is derived from no other principle than our observation of the veracity of human testimony, and of the usual conformity of facts to the reports of witnesses' which he cites as: Selby-Bigge (1902, p.88)

10. Philipse (2012. pp.321-22)

11. Hay (1994, p.21)

12. Philipse (2012. pp.332-33)

13. I include Christianity here among the great monotheistic faiths because it seems to claim that no other gods exist than the Christian Trinity.

14. E.g. 2 Pet. 1:20-21, 'First of all you must understand this, that no prophecy of Scripture is a matter of one's own interpretation, because no prophecy ever came by the impulse of

man, but men moved by the Holy Spirit spoke from God.'

15. *Cf.* Segal, (2002). And the following for its accessibility: Heiser (2004).

16. Peterson & VanArragon (2004. pp.154-55)

17. Oppy (2006. p.350, n.4)

18. *Cf.* Kwan (2009. pp.498-552)

19. '[Interpretation] is absolutely essential to there occurring a perceptual experience at all....We are not passive recipients of ready-made representations of our environment; rather, stimuli from that environment must be processed by various interpretive mechanisms before they can have any significance for us' – Davis (1989. p.149). As cited in Kwan (2009. p.505)

20. For instance, perhaps the simplicity of a hypothesis is to be understood in terms of how many auxiliary hypotheses it requires to explain the data: the fewer it requires the simpler it is. On this, polytheism is a simpler hypothesis than monotheism since polytheism can take our data (religious experiences of different objects) at face value, while monotheism would have to postulate auxiliary hypotheses to explain why only one god is appearing under numerous guises. Perhaps simplicity is just the amount of information contained in a hypothesis. On this, it's entirely unclear whether polytheism is more complex than monotheism since monotheism could make up for the number of deities posited in polytheism by the complex powers it ascribes to this deity.

21. Wilkerson (2014. p.169)

Chapter 4: Are the Gods Good?

1. Aquinas, *Summa Theologica* P. 1, Q.1, A. 8 in Pegis (1948, p.14)

2. Moreland & Craig (2003. p.586)

3. *Ibid.* pp.586-87

4. *Cf.* Schellenberg, (2006) for an example of a deductive evidential problem of evil.

5. Skeptical-theism is standardly defined as the conjunction of the following theses:

    'ST1: We have no good reason for thinking that the possible goods we know of are representative of the possible goods there are.

    ST2: We have no good reason for thinking that the possible evils we know of are representative of the possible evils there are.

    ST3: We have no good reason for thinking that the entailment relations we know of between possible goods and the permission of possible evils are representative of the entailment relations there are between possible goods and the permission of possible evils.' – Bergmann & Rea (2005: pp.241–251)

    To hold at least one of these claims is moderate skeptical-theism.

6. We needn't understand this sense of responsibility in terms of a feeling; it could just as well be accounted for as an awareness, or even belief.

Chapter 5: Unanswered Questions

1. Baggett & Walls. (2011)
2. Smith (2001. p.48-49)
3. *The New Jerome Biblical Commentary.* (1999. p.108)

Select Bibliography

Alexander, Eben. *Proof of Heaven: A Neurosurgeon's Journey into the Afterlife*. New York, NY: Simon & Schuster, 2012.

An Enquiry Concerning Human Understanding, ed. L. A. Selby-Bigge. Oxford: Oxford University Press, 1902, section 88

Audi, Robert. *Epistemology: a Contemporary Introduction to the Theory of Knowledge*. 2nd ed. London: Routledge, 2007.

Aquinas Thomas, *Summa Theologica* 2nd revised edition. Translated by English Dominican Fathers. New York: Benzinger. Available online: http://newadvent.org/summa. Accessed April 5, 2014.

Baggett, David, and Jerry L. Walls. *Good God: The Theistic Foundations of Morality*. New York: Oxford UP, 2011.

Barry Loewer in McLaughlin, Brian P., and Jonathan D. Cohen. *Contemporary Debates in Philosophy of Mind*. Malden, MA: Blackwell Pub., 2007.

Bergmann, Michael and Rea, Michael. 'In Defence of Sceptical Theism: A Reply to Almeida and Oppy'. *Australasian Journal of Philosophy* 83.2, (2005): pp.241–251

Davis, C. *The Evidential Force of Religious Experience*. Oxford: Clarendon Press, 1989.

Damascus, John. *Exposition of the Orthodox Faith*. Translated by E.W. Watson and L. Pullan. From Nicene and Post-Nicene Fathers, Second Series, Vol. 9. Edited by Philip Schaff and Henry Wace. (Buffalo, NY: Christian Literature Publishing Co., 1899) Available online: http://www.newadvent.org/fathers/33041.htm..Accessed April 5, 2014.

Exposition of the Orthodox Faith, Book 1, Chapter 5.

Feser, Edward. *Aquinas: A Beginner's Guide*. Oxford: Oneworld, 2009.

Godwin, Jocelyn. *The Pagan Dream of the Renaissance*. Red Wheel

Wiser, 2005.

Greer, John M. *A World Full of Gods: An Inquiry Into Polytheism*. Tuscon, Arizona: ADF, 2005.

Hatcher, William. *The Bahá'í Faith*. San Francisco: Harper & Row, 1985.

Hay, D. (1994) 'The biology of God: what is the current status of Hardy's hypothesis?' *International Journal for the Psychology of Religion* 4:1, 1–23.

Heiser, Michael S. 'The Divine Council in Late Canonical and Non-Canonical Second Temple Jewish Literature.' Diss. UNIVERSITY OF WISCONSIN-MADISON, 2004.

Huemer, Michael. *Ethical Intuitionism*. Basingstoke: Palgrave Macmillan, 2005.

Huemer, Michael. *Skepticism and the Veil of Perception*. Lanham, MD: Rowman & Littlefield, 2001.

Kwan, Kai-Man. 'The Arguments From Religious Experience'. *Blackwell Companion to Natural Theology*. Chichester, U.K.: Wiley-Blackwell, 2009.

Lewis, D. *Parts of Classes*, Oxford: Blackwell. 1991.

Moreland, James Porter, and William Lane, Craig. *Philosophical Foundations for a Christian Worldview*. Downers Grove, IL: InterVarsity, 2003.

Murray, Alexzander S. *Who's Who in Mythology: A Classic Guide to the Ancient World*. New York: Random House, 1998.

Myers, Brendan. *The Earth, the Gods and the Soul: A History of Pagan Philosophy from the Iron Age to the 21st Century*. Washington: Moon, 2013.

Oderberg, David. *Real Essentialism*. New York: Routledge, 2007.

Oppy, Graham. *Arguing about Gods*. New York: Cambridge UP, 2006.

Peterson, Michael L., and Raymond J. VanArragon.*Contemporary Debates in Philosophy of Religion*. Malden, MA: Blackwell Pub., 2004.

Pegis, Thomas, and Anton C. *Introduction to St. Thomas Aquinas*.

New York: Modern Library, 1948.

Philipse, Herman. *God in the Age of Science? A Critique of Religious Reason.* Oxford: Oxford UP, 2012.

Schellenberg, John L. *Divine Hiddenness and Human Reason: With a New Preface.* Ithaca (N.Y.): Cornell UP, 2006.

Segal, Alan F. *Two Powers in Heaven: Early Rabbinic Reports About Christianity and Gnosticism.* N.p.: Brill Academic, 2002.

Smith, Mark S. *The Origins of Biblical Monotheism: Israel's Polytheistic Background and the Ugaritic Texts.* Oxford: Oxford University Press, 2001.

Swinburne, Richard. *The Existence of God.* Oxford: Oxford UP. 2004.

Taliaferro, C.; Draper, P.; Quinn, P.L. *A Companion to Philosophy of Religion.* John Wiley & Sons, 2010.

The New Jerome Biblical Commentary. Englewood Cliffs, NJ: Prentice Hall, 1999.

Wall, G. *Religious Experience and Religious Belief.* Lanham, MD: University Press of America, 1995.

Waterfield, Robin.*The First Philosophers: The Presocratics and Sophists.* Oxford: Oxford UP, 2000.

William James, *The Varieties of Religious Experience.* New York: Modern Library, 1902.

Willis, Roy G. *World Mythology: The Illustrated Guide.* Oxford: Oxford UP, 2006.

Wilkerson, W.D. *Walking With The Gods: Modern People Talk about Deities, Faith, and Recreating Ancient Religious Traditions.* Sand Springs, OK: Connaissance Sankofa Media, Inc. 2014.

BOOKS

Iff Books is interested in ideas and reasoning. It publishes
material on science, philosophy and law. Iff Books aims to work
with authors and titles that augment our understanding of the
human condition, society and civilisation, and the world or
universe in which we live.